The Moment
That Matters

*restore balance to your home, your life
and your environment through awareness
and responsibility...*

ERIC DOWSETT

National Library of Australia: ISBN 0 646 3323 2

    1. Dowsing   2. Personal Growth   3. The Mind   4. Spirituality
    5. Environmental Issues.

Published in 1997 By: Eric Dowsett
                          P.O. Box 751 Maroochydore
                          Qld. 4558 Australia

Author:	Eric Dowsett
Book Design:	Eric Dowsett
Cover Photo:	Karen Dambrauskas © 1991
Author Photo:	Karen Dambrauskas
Editing:	Alleyn Best

Printed by: Bermuda Print Pty. Ltd., Victoria, Australia

To all those who would be free
May this work help you achieve your goal

CONTENTS

- A Personal Start
- Energy Is The Source
- Perceiving Energy
- The Physical Form of Energy
- Beyond Physical Energy
- The Unseen Energy Fields
- The Higher Energy

- Magnetic Energies
- A Webbed Energy Field
- All Life Is Consciousness
- The Underlying Holoverse
- Our Stressed Environment
- Being Aware

- Finding The Cause Of Stress
- Fear And Stress
- Feeling Stress Energies
- Geo-Pathic Stress
- Water
- Dowsing Water Energy
- Inherited Energies

ACKNOWLEDGMENTS

I would like to thank all those that knew this work was within me, their support has helped make this book possible.

Pat Kaye and Lloyd Williams for the haven that allowed me to put the thoughts down on paper.

Alleyn Best for helping turn those thoughts into a finished book.

Barry and Judith Williams for their belief in this work and the assistance in publishing the book.

The love of my friends.

FOREWORD

Every so often a book comes along that is designed to clarify - as well as educate. Eric Dowsett has worked in his field of study and practice for numerous years, helping a great many people. His is not a dogmatic 'take it or leave it' approach, but one of gently and gradually introducing his subject. We all think we know about the physical body, and we all think we know about spirituality, and again, we think we know about Earth energies, but how many of us ever make the connection between all of these? For most people these are vague, conceptual, gray areas; things best not thought about too often. We believe our lives to be separate from the planet Earths, and that our physical life has little to do with our inner spirituality. Seldom do we focus on the greater reality of the connection of all life, of all energies, of all thinking, to the whole.

The body we live in, the house we live in, and the area we live in all affect us. We are not isolated, biological mobile units; we are a connection of energy fields woven in with the universe, the Earth, humanity, our thinking, all as a greater whole.

The Moment That Matters offers clarity and explanation. It takes away those 'gray' areas. As you read you find yourself muttering, "But of course," "Ah ha," "I see," "So that's how it works," and all the while nodding enthusiastically. Enjoy it, I did.

Michael J. Roads
Author: Talking with Nature, Journey into Nature
             Journey into Oneness, Into a Timeless Realm
             Simple is Powerful, Getting There, a novel.

PREFACE

This book has been based on my feelings of how things are. These feelings have been built up around practical experience and direct knowing as I have gone deeper into the search for the self. There is something else there that will not be denied, a knowing at the very core of my being that, given the opportunity to express itself, begins to stir and awaken like the sleeping dragon. This something is the structure upon which all else fits, the foundations for the building blocks that are the accumulated experiences of life.

For the moment we can call this something the *seed*. Ultimately we may all have the same origins: God, Allah, Jehovah, Divine Consciousness, Prime Creator – call it what you feel you need to. As this *seed* on its journey of discovery gathers more and more experiences and becomes attached to those experiences, the knowledge of its origins becomes more and more obscure.

For many travellers on life's path this *New Age* is bringing more confusion than clarity. Opportunities for personal growth seem to exist in more areas now than for many years. Books, lectures, workshops and healers have sprung up like mushrooms after a storm. The boom in the search for the meaning of life, evolution and ascension is unprecedented. Something is obviously happening for many souls across the planet as we head toward the next millennium.

My dowsing experiences and listening to my inner promptings (intuition) and observing the life experiences of those around me make me increasingly concerned that many people are chasing shadows in the hopeful expectation that those shadows will lead them from the darkness of their confusions.

Shadows may hold out the promise of a new reality but in actual fact they only serve to ensnare the seeker in the confusion of Maya: the illusory, sensory world.

For many years I have held workshops and seminars dealing with the relationships we maintain with our environment, be it the physical environment, the technological or the metaphysical. These workshops encourage a greater degree of self-responsibility in all that we think, say and do. They show that who we think we are affects the environment in which we live.

I have written this book in response to those people who encouraged me to "put down on paper" what I have spoken about in my lectures and workshops. It does not claim to contain all the pieces to the puzzle. There are many books that contain parts of the puzzle, but no one book contains it all. Hopefully I will be able to add sequels which contain new insights and understandings as they occur.

May the words and ideas contained in these pages help to further enlighten you and guide you away from the seductions of Maya and place you at the door to your personal Nirvana.

Thus have I heard...

CASE STUDIES

All of the people who have attended the workshops around which this book was written all have one thing in common; a desire to improve their health and lifestyle.

Workshop participants come from all walks of life; teachers, doctors, psychologists, homeopaths, healers, farmers, accountants, school age children, the employed and unemployed, computer programmers, technicians, housewives. Anyone in fact that is interested in moving beyond current limiting perceptions of the 'self'.

Employing the many levels of the ancient art of 'Dowsing', as explained in the text, we are able to tap into knowledge and wisdom that would otherwise be beyond our reach. With this knowledge and wisdom comes an ability to consciously co-create our reality, this leads to healing self, others and our environment.

The following anecdotes and case studies come from people who have attended one or more workshops. They are meant as examples of the healing potential available to us all, without reading the rest of the book however, they may be difficult to comprehend and leave many questions unanswered.

Dowsing on Personal Health:

Jim, a Homeopath working in Melbourne has been keeping records of patients treated using the techniques learnt in the workshop in conjunction with traditional homeopathic treatments.

A 75 year old male with prostate cancer which had progressed to bone cancer had lost the will to become involved in day to day affairs. His energy was low and he had had no sex drive for six months prior to diagnosis of the prostate cancer. The prostrate cancer was diagnosed two and a half years ago. Every day he would settle in front of the television and shut out the rest of the world. The life threatening nature of his disease had robbed him of the will to live.

"My patient was not present at the time I applied these techniques and I was relying on feedback from his wife to indicate changes in his condition.

The following day I had a call from his wife, she said that there was quite a noticeable change in her husband's behaviour. He was working once again around the house doing odd jobs that before had been too much for him and no longer sat in front of the television all day. His energy levels had risen and he appeared to be much happier.

Two weeks later I was told of other improvements the most notable of which was a return to a healthy sex life (an average of three times a fortnight) within days of the treatment and which persists to this day. After a break of two and a half years without sex this was a most remarkable turnaround.

This client's sense of wellbeing changed dramatically after the treatment and is maintained to this day (seven months after initial treatment using these techniques).

There had been no change in other treatment to this patient, the improvement being so abrupt following this treatment I can come to no other conclusion. This treatment had a profound effect on this man's sense of wellbeing."

Having Trouble Selling Your House?:

…"My name is Nick and I have been dowsing now for about 12 months. I would like to share the following story that happened six months ago and which demonstrates the effects that can be achieved with a pendulum, an L rod and an open mind.

One weekend my family and I were visiting a friend of the family who had been trying to sell his house for approximately three months. Every Sunday he would have an open day and people would come to look at the house but no one would ever stay for more than five minutes. I should mention that his wife had died six months earlier from cancer.

On this particular weekend I spoke to our friend about dowsing his house to clear any negative energies that may have been affecting the sale of the house. After a brief discussion and demonstration of the pendulum, our friend decided that he would like to have his house cleared. It was agreed that I would come back the following day to do the work.

When I arrived the next day I felt a little apprehensive, as if someone did not want me there, but I proceeded with the work anyway. The first question I asked was if there were any entities that needed to be cleared from this house and I received a positive reply from the pendulum. Then, armed with my L rod, I proceeded to look for the location of the entity. From the front door I was led on a merry chase, first up the stairs to the master bedroom and then back down and through a number of other rooms before stopping in the bedroom of the youngest child, Samantha. (This room also contained the mothers bed which

Samantha now used). Once the L rod had led me to the centre of the bed I used the pendulum to determine if it was right and proper to help this entity move on from our physical world and on to the next. Again I received a positive reply from the pendulum and so began the clearing.

During the clearing I was exposed to two very strong emotions. At first I could feel a great sadness and I understood that this woman was very sad and didn't want to leave her children. Later there was intense joy as she finally understood that moving on was the right thing to do for both herself and her loved ones. This whole clearing process took about fifteen minutes from start to finish but by the end I was feeling quite strange, this feeling lasted for about two hours.

During the same afternoon when the house was open for inspection there were two couples who both stayed for about half an hour, one of the couples expressed an interest in buying the property. The house sold four weeks later. During the week after the clearing our friend had a friend ask him what had changed about the house noting that the house now felt lighter".

Healing the Land:

Fay, from Brisbane started learning energy dowsing about one year ago. Her story is a little different, demonstrating the broad nature of the work.

..."The experience that stands out most vividly was when I was dowsing for geological faults on my property. There was a problem area that had never responded to fertiliser, gypsum or even covering with turf. This area was compacted with heavy clay and rocks and had no grass cover, the trees were sickly, straggling gums.

Using the L rod I located a pressure ridge running east to west. I then used the pendulum to confirm my findings with the L rod. I then asked if it was in order for me to release the pressure in the ridge and restore harmony to the area. Upon receiving an affirmative answer I asked for the healing to begin.

The next moment I felt as if I was actually in the earth and could see the pressure and stress that was being exerted along the pressure line. I began to loosen and free the earth and rocks all the way along.

Since then, this once stressed area has started to accumulate top soil and grass. The trees are showing more foliage and even flowers. Some wild life (mostly possums) have returned to the area.

To the best of my knowledge there is no other reason for the sudden change to the area.

Understanding and Releasing Grief:

The following story comes from a teacher in Armidale, Northern New South Wales.

Not long after doing the workshop in March 1995, I had to unblock a sewerage pipe. I grabbed my trusty piece of wire and proceeded to locate the pipe. Not only was I able to locate the sewerage line, but also the inspection plates and determined how deep they were. It saved me a great deal of digging and a lot of time.

Despite my continued success in divining pipes, water and physical phenomenon it is dowsing on people's energy fields that captures my interest.

On one occasion, I was asked to dowse on a young woman who had lost her much loved father a month or so earlier. She was frightened and unable to rest. Her sleep was interrupted by realistic dreams that haunted her and played on her mind all the time.

During dowsing, areas of disturbance were found in all energy fields. The young lady related closely to the feelings and sensations that I felt and relayed to her. The overall feeling of the whole session was one of letting go.

Several months later, this young lady expressed to me her dramatic reduction in fear, which occurred in the days following the dowsing. She became intuitive and was able to gain great personal strength from the dreams which had previously haunted her.

The young woman attributed the shift in her well-being directly to the dowsing.

Awareness and use of the dowsing has brought about personal growth in my life. I have acquired a great respect for my path in life and the paths of others".

Improving Business Profitability:

From a baker in suburban Melbourne comes a story of a different application of the work

The bakery has always had an environment of happiness, harmony and success - however I have had an awareness of one area that was an energy 'drain'.

Impressed with the results of Eric's energy clearing in our house, we invited him to work on our business. One consultation effectively increased profits and harmony, whilst clearing the energy block.

If you are willing to begin to take responsibility for your own reality I urge you to approach and embrace these ideas.

One

Energy is All

A Personal Start

The journey, for me, began who knows when. I am not a psychic with clear visions of the past. I have no distinct memory of 'past lives' even if I were to believe in 'past' lives. I do 'know', however, that there is much more to life and living than meets the eye.

As a youngster I was very sensitive and shy, a little different from my friends. Try as I would to fit in, something held me apart. Early in my teens I recall questioning the headmaster during a religious instruction class, "why, if you are teaching us about religion did you not include the teachings of the Buddha?" Where this idea came from I did not know. I was duly ignored and another opportunity passed by for me to understand more of who and what I was/am. Later I was to speak confidently with Buddhist monks on the Dharma, never having read anything on Buddhism.

At the time I just accepted this knowledge and did not question where it came from or why it was coming out of my head. Fortunately, between then and now, I have had the opportunity to understand why I have this inbuilt, accessible and quite refined knowledge.

Energy is the Source

All of my talks, lectures, seminars and workshops start from the same point, namely an awareness that all is energy. Our body, like all other bodies, be they animal, vegetable or mineral, are forms constructed of matter which was, is and always will be energy. Applying this notion of energy to ourselves and our total environment can be explained by quantum physics but most of us tend to get lost in that world. For most of us, energy is electricity, generated by wind, water, sun or fossil fuels to produce power. Petrol provides the energy to keep our motor vehicles moving; electricity provides the energy that keeps our society operating. These forms of energy upon which our society is based are relatively new to planet earth. Primarily we extract non-renewable energy from the planet but this results in polluting the environment at the same time. Technology, its benefits and downside, will be looked at later in the book.

We are told by the mass media of the 20th century that energy from the sun, as vital as it is to life as we know it on planet Earth, can burn your skin. We are also told that the ultra violet range of the sun's light (for light you can also read energy) can, if you are not careful, cause skin cancer. The sun is one mighty energy producer around which our earth revolves once every 365 1/4 days. Without this sun, life just would not exist as we currently experience it. Light is an obvious manifestation of the sun's energy; heat is another obvious part of this energy. Yet light is not simply just 'light'; it is a broad range of frequencies that are a necessary part of our evolution and well-being.

As an example of this evolution, consider a tiny carrot seed that contains the information package of a carrot. When this seed is planted in the energy field of soil and then more energy in the form of water and sunlight is applied to it, the memory inherent in the seed's nature, namely that of a carrot, is triggered. The seed sprouts and with continued input of the right amounts of energy, not too much nor too little, the seed takes that energy and transforms it into a carrot which is energy in another form. We then pick the carrot and eat it. By eating it we take the stored and transformed energy of the carrot and use that energy to fuel our cells and maintain physical life. All life is sustained in a similar fashion. By absorbing and utilising the energy of plant or animal life (which in turn received its energy from the sun) we are able to support the life of the human form.

Energy is all around us. Everything in fact is energy in one form or another. However eating or drinking food is not the only way we absorb energy. The very energy of the earth itself provides a necessary source of energy. The sun's ultra violet rays provide life supporting energy. We are constantly involved in an exchange of energies on many levels.

Perceiving Energy

The scientific mind has reduced us and all matter to sub-atomic particles. If we go down their path we would find that we do not even exist in physical terms, for the spaces between the minute atom's nucleus and its even smaller neutrons and protons appear to be full of ... nothing! We appear solid, but, as we shall see, this 'solidity' is based on the tools which we use to 'see' and is not the reality of the matter. A neutrino for example, which is the smallest of particles (or wave form) would pass through us as easily as we pass through a cloud in an aeroplane.

Our perception of our world is relative to the tools which we use to perceive that world. A flower seen through the eyes of a bird or an insect is entirely different to our accepted perception of the flower. A spider's web, glorious to us in the early morning dew, appears totally different to the insects it is designed to entrap. A chameleon, with eyes that swivel through 360 degrees sees the world in a way that we could not even begin to imagine. The examples are numerous to print here to show that we see and interpret our environment with specific tools designed to make survival of the physical form as secure as possible. This perception creates our reality.

The Physical Form of Energy

Our physical form is comprised of cells, which are in turn made up of atoms and sub atomic particles, all of which have a particular frequency of oscillation. A cell in the bone in the foot for example, is differentiated from an optical nerve by its frequency. It follows that we are a complex collection of different frequencies of atoms and sub atomic particles, all held in check by the information contained in the DNA and RNA. This is a little simplistic but will be enlarged on later.

Our personal energy system is an electric field which is primarily direct current (DC). This is an important point as we shall discover when we look at our relationship with the earth and with technological energy fields. The brain and the nervous system are exceptions to this rule and operate in an alternating current (AC) energy field.

We have a physical form that is composed of atoms and sub atomic particles that is purely energy manifesting itself in a particular form. That form is supplemented and added to by the information contained in the collective consciousness of the species [1]. It has been found that many different species contain the same DNA so there appears to be something else at work here that differentiates a human bone cell from that of an emu.

Accepting the fact that we are energy manifesting as human beings we must then look at our world and see it as energy, manifesting itself as our reality according to our perceptions.

Beyond Physical Energy

The approach that I have taken to increase my personal awareness of these other energy fields has been wide and far reaching while at the same time realising that my view of the world is limited by my own limited perceptions of self. By starting with a view of the body as an energy field it is possible to use this examination point as a foundation on which to build a greater overview.

We are not isolated or self contained energy beings. Rather we are interactive, interdependent unique personalities who exist within a greater framework of personalities and energy fields, many of which we are not aware. Our very existence on planet Earth is dependant upon a multitude of energy fields, some obvious, others becoming more so and there are still more such energy fields that most of us have long forgotten.

It is obvious to us that we have a physical body. We can see it, touch it, hear it and smell it. The physical body is real and well within the ability of our senses to comprehend. This body is energy, highly complex and very well designed but energy nonetheless. Furthermore we know that the body does not end with the physical aspect, a concept accepted for centuries in the Hindu teachings. We have what can be called subtle bodies. An easy way to understand and accept these subtle bodies is to refer again to our body as energy. Our eyes and nervous system have been designed with physical survival in mind. Whatever is unnecessary for survival has not, on a conscious level, been included. By means of our five physical senses we are able to see or recognise certain energy fields that are vibrating low enough to appear as matter of a dense nature.

The Unseen Energy Fields

Some beings can see an energy pattern radiating out from the body's electrical field. This pattern is known as the aura. However it is not one of the subtle bodies that we shall be looking at here. The Auric field is of a frequency a little out of the range of most people's perception and is a result of the electrical energy generated by the physical body. The subtle bodies I refer to are higher frequencies yet again and certainly beyond physical sight. Subtle bodies are, in order of increasing frequency: the etheric body; the emotional or astral body; the mental or causal body; the spiritual body and one that I have named the GAIA field, after James Lovelocks' coining of the Greek Goddess' name for a holistic earth. This GAIA field, sometimes referred to as the nature conscious field, is a link between the unmanifest and third dimensional reality, or a jumping off point, as it were, into earth space/time. As the bridge between soul and physical form the GAIA field is a fundamental level of awareness.

The etheric body as such is the blueprint for the physical body, comprising a complex web or grid pattern. Our etheric body is approximately 50 cm from the physical form. The etheric "web" is the final stage of the unseen energy fields or subtle bodies where information is stored that builds and maintains the physical form.

It is important that this energy field or "web" is in good condition since any disturbances in the etheric field may sooner or later manifest as physical disease. Energy as information passes through all the subtle energy fields into the physical via the seven major chakras, or energy vortexes. Much has been written already on the chakras and I leave it to any interested reader to follow up this topic [2].

The Higher Energy

Moving higher up the frequency range we find the emotional, or astral body. This energy field stores our emotions. Our desires too are contained in this energy pattern. When we are disturbed by trauma or a particular belief pattern (which is stored in the next field, the mental or causal body) the energy held in the emotional body can disrupt the physical form as well as affect our emotional health and stability. The emotional body plays an important role in the spiritual evolution of our species. It seems that without the feeling aspects of our being which we access through the emotional body we cannot evolve to a higher state of consciousness.

Higher again up the scale of energies there is the mental or causal body where all information about who we are, who we were and who we will be is stored. Our potential is found in this energy field. Our perceptions, positive and negative are also contained here as well as the ability to change those perceptions. This field can be likened to a library storing memories of our total experiences in this physical form.

The spiritual field contains fundamental information about who we are and the reasons we perceive as we do. This field can hold patterns of information relating to our ability to receive and interpret higher consciousness or 'spiritual' information.

The GAIA or nature consciousness field as mentioned earlier seems to be the bridge between energy and matter and appears to contain information of a very basic level.

There are other fields, one in particular that interests me beyond the GAIA field. Only twice have I accessed this field and the information centred around what I call 'Home'. It seems as though beyond all that we could possibly imagine there lies yet greater areas of ourselves that have yet to be rediscovered.

Overall it is important to understand that as energy bodies we are in constant communication with all other energies and that there are no barriers that isolate us from the rest of creation.

Two

The Earth's Energy Levels

Magnetic Energies

As human beings, our species has evolved over millennia in the natural energy field of the earth. So let us take a closer look at this earth of ours.

The earth is far from being the solid object of our collective perceptions due to the slow rate of vibration of the atoms that make up the earth. Our planet earth is just energy, that is, matter of a denser nature than water or air, but matter nonetheless. Higher frequency energy patterns, for example radioactive energy, pass as easily through the earth as a knife slices through soft butter.

If you studied simple physics at school you discovered the energy field of a bar magnet by placing a piece of paper over the magnet and sprinkling iron filings onto the paper. The patterns which the magnetic field formed were represented by the formation of the iron filings. But our interest here is the magnetic field that runs through the earth. These narrow bands of geo-magnetic energy in the natural state of positive polarity are beneficial and support life on earth.

This magnetic field has two components, the first being the frequency of the field as measured in cycles per second, (Hertz or Hz). The second is the intensity of the field which is measured in milli Gauss, a common unit of energy measurement for a magnetic field. (It is not my intention to get too technical. Most people whom I have worked with look lost and a little vague when I refer to milli Gauss and Herz). These measurements serve tō explain the relationship between the fields and the affects they have on the physical, mental and emotional forms but are of little concern for the broader picture presented here.

It is important to be aware that the geo-magnetic field of the earth is a direct current (DC) field. This is a naturally occurring energy pattern and is the one that humanity has evolved in these past millennia. DC fields alternate their intensity by giving a pulse frequency directly proportional to wave amplitude, whereas alternating current (AC) alternates polarity (in the case of the power supply to our homes and industry from 0 to 50 Hz). It is important to note this difference when we compare electro-magnetic fields and geo-magnetic fields (Geo, from the earth and electro, in this case, from the domestic and industrial power supply).

Keep in mind that we are ourselves energy bodies composed of a multitude of different, highly exact, frequencies and that for the most part our systems are of a DC nature. The energy forces of the geo-magnetic nature of the earth are required by the physical forms that inhabit the earth in order to grow and evolve. It is important that our environment be in a stable state for us to grow in a healthy and happy manner. The geo-magnetic field is primarily of a positive polarity, the compass points north, with north being the positive end of the bar magnet that is the earth.

Where this natural flow is undisturbed – by either naturally occurring phenomena, such as earthquakes, volcanic action or plate movement, landslide etc, or man made actions, such as railway lines, airports, mines, quarries etc – it has been found that such areas are healthy and beneficial to mankind.

A Webbed Energy Field

As mentioned previously, the earth's magnetic field has two components, a frequency and an intensity. Direct current (DC) frequency is the frequency compatible with the human body. Research has shown that the body, any body be it human, animal, vegetable or mineral is composed of cells, atoms and sub-atomic particles. A cell takes on a particular job e.g. the cell of a nerve ending in the little finger of a human moves from an undifferentiated state, meaning the cell was available to fulfil any task required, into a differentiated state, that of the nerve ending in the little finger [3]. It is my belief that it does this at the request of the etheric energy field or web of 'invisible' meridians known by the Hindu as the nadis, in conjunction with the DNA of the individual. This etheric energy field acts like a master blueprint for the manifestation of the physical, so much so that any disturbance in the etheric leads to the 'incorrect' manifestation of cellular frequency, with resultant dis-ease.

The immune system, which is our personal health watch dog, will automatically wall off or destroy any cell with an 'incorrect' frequency, i.e. an unhealthy cell. The immune system's effectiveness is limited by the number of stress factors in the life of the individual. What does it mean to have a cell vibrating at an incorrect frequency? How does it happen and what are the results? The results are obvious manifestations of dis-ease, be it in the physical body, the mental or emotional bodies (psychiatric disturbance).

All parts of our body, constructed from differentiated cells, have specific and optimum frequencies required to maintain good health. Where the frequency is disturbed, by whatever cause, a breakdown in good health invariably follows. There are a number of factors that affect the stability of the individual cellular frequencies, dependant upon the immune system's efficiency and the individual's physiology.

As energy bodies that live in an energy environment we cannot help but be affected by the environment, at least by our perception of that environment. The whole area of memory and perceptions will be looked at in detail after we have explored a few foundations in the physical world.

All Life is Conscious

Our physical home, planet Earth, is a living, conscious being. All matter is energy. Breaking that down further, all energy is atomic particles, each with a specific job manifesting in our physical world. What decided upon the cellular structure of granite as opposed to sandstone? We know that both are rocks with very different characteristics defined by the different molecular structure. But where did the instructions come from that differentiated the cellular frequencies in the first place? This, I believe, is consciousness, the consciousness of the rocks. Consciousness extends to all living matter. The rocks are alive in that they have a blueprint, or energetic pattern that stays true to form and continues to produce a specific type of rock. Consciousness varies as life varies. There are more complex consciousnesses, such as man and the primates, whales and dolphins and down the scale we go from animals to plants to microbes, all having some degree of consciousness. This perception of our reality is fundamental to understanding the part we play on this planet.

Difficult as it may be to accept, all that takes form (shape) in our reality can be seen in many different ways, depending upon the characteristics and requirements of the observer. As explained earlier, a fly or a chameleon, an eagle or an owl, a dolphin or a bat all experience life on this planet in a different way. We humans have our own way of viewing the world. We have senses that interpret data in a specific way. Physicist David Bohm enlarges upon the concept of the hologram[4], extending it to include all life as a moving hologram or 'holomovement'. Simply put, a hologram is an image captured by a laser which is a beam of coherent light (as opposed to the broad spectrum light that we get from the sun), that appears to have three dimensional qualities. When this image is captured on the photographic plate it differs enormously from an ordinary photographic negative. Instead of portraying a likeness of the object 'photographed', the holographic image displays a complex series of concentric circles. Picture it as the effect you get when a pebble is thrown into a still pond and the ripples move outward in ever widening circles. Now imagine a handful of pebbles thrown into the pond. Instead of one focus from which the ripples emanate we have many, thus creating complex patterns where each ripple collides with the next to form multiple crests and troughs. This effect is known as interfering wave patterns. Imagine this pond now being frozen in time: this would give us a picture similar to that of a hologram, a stationary, three dimensional image. Obviously our lives are far more complex than that image, so now we 'unfreeze' the pond and allow the ripples to continue, all the time adding more pebbles to the pond to keep the image moving, altering and dynamic. This becomes the holomovement that David Bohm talks about.

The Underlying Holomovement

The amazing feature of a holographic plate, as opposed to an ordinary photographic plate is that if you were to break the holographic plate into many thousands of pieces, each part would, with some possible loss of quality, display the whole. As parts of this unfolding holomovement we, like the broken holographic plate, contain the information of the whole. For many of us this may be the first time we have even attempted to look at the universe in such a way. Certainly the difficult part is accessing all of the information instead of the tiny part we have adopted as our personal reality. As physical beings we have evolved in a three dimensional world where survival has been a major factor. The result is that our nervous and sensory systems have developed a particular way of observing this world.

As a basis of any reality we care to imagine, accept that there is an underlying field of interfering wave patterns, the holoverse. By applying our unique sensory system in order to translate those interfering wave patterns we can see physical forms that we are then able to recognise as our accepted reality. Life, as we commonly believe it to be, did not exist before we applied our sensory systems to the problem of interpreting the data which initially manifested as interfering wave forms, all interacting with each other to form unique, ever changing patterns. At least life did not exist in the forms that we are comfortable with. So, as with the holographic plate where a laser of similar coherency is required to be applied to the plate in order to make 'sense' of the patterns, we need our own sense systems, tuned in a specific and particular way, to make sense of the energy forms, the cosmic soup, within which we exist as human beings.

Now, how does this affect the immune system's function and consequently our ability to maintain good health? Back to the pond: if a series of pebbles are thrown at frequent intervals into the pond a particular reality will unfold. If a maverick pebble finds its way into the pond then all subsequent realities have been affected, in one way or another – the proverbial 'spanner in the works'. For the moment, imagine that the random pebble is a disturbance in our physical 'external' environment.

Our Stressed Environment

As explained earlier, the earth's magnetic field is composed of particular frequencies and an intensities. Looking closely at the frequency, remembering that this energy is of a direct current nature and is compatible with the human body, we find that various earth frequencies resonate, or are identical with, various frequencies found in our body. Whilst our physical body lives in an environment that is harmonious, the geo-physical environment in this case (the earth and energies associated with the earth), and the individual cells in our bodies are in a comfortable state. When however the earth's magnetic field has been disturbed, be it by a man-made or a naturally occurring disturbance, then that specific field takes on a negative polarity. This disturbance subsequently becomes yet another factor applying stress to the body.

Over a period of time, dependant upon the strength of the individual's immune system and other stress factors in that person's life, the stress in the environment can adversely affect a person's health to the point where a physical manifestation of dis-ease may occur. Many patients of allopathic or 'alternative' treatments may get relief from the manifesting symptoms of the stress by these treatments. But if the person's environment is adding to or causing states of distress then no amount of treatment can solve the problem. Whilst we seek rest and recuperation in a 'sick' environment any treatments will be purely on a symptomatic level and consequently the cause will continue to be present, thereby aggravating the condition of the patient.

Areas of geo-pathic stress [5] of greater intensity will of course have a greater and more rapid impact upon people living or spending time within such areas than in low level areas. There are many factors that need to be taken into account, hence the difficulty amongst many to accept this proposal. Geo-pathic stress is but one of a number of factors in our total environment, and, as we shall see later, all factors, or more precisely our response to those factors, can be traced back to one cause.

The aim of this work is to seek fundamental cause wherever possible. Change of a lasting beneficial nature can only be found when the fundamental cause for distress is healed. Whilst the 'established order' seeks to find solutions to the woes of the world based on the paradigms that created those woes, we will only sink deeper into the mire of confusion and illusion.

Being Aware

A constant theme in this book is awareness. As we develop awareness of the real nature of ourselves and our environment so we become empowered to consciously affect that environment. There is nothing new to the fact that we are affecting our environment, but what is different and very exciting is the possibility of 'conscious participation'. Basing a reality on love and not greed, fear or ignorance is a powerful path to a sustainable future for humanity on planet earth.

If you knew that the energy generated by the earth over which you had placed your bed was affecting your health in a negative way would you leave your bed there? Awareness becomes a key, a key to opening a door that leads beyond the current limitations of mind and body. Whilst we still have a body we need to take care of that vehicle but not become totally preoccupied with it. Until our awareness reaches a point where we are able to transcend limitations of the physical we will need to take steps to reduce the stress to which our bodies, physically, emotionally and mentally are currently being subjected.

If we fail to awaken to our environment, especially our relationship to that environment, the state of dynamic tension that we generate in our ignorance builds up, somewhat like an elastic band that is constantly being stretched so that sooner or later it will break or we must let go. When that happens the energy attempts, rapidly, to return to a balanced state. In the process of restoring balance, the physical, emotional or mental bodies, possibly the spiritual, will go through a healing crisis. The extent of the healing crisis will correspond to the degree that the elastic band was stretched, that is, to the inner tension we created. This healing crisis can be so severe that we cannot deal with the changes effectively and so the body dies.

Most states of sickness or dis-ease are healing crises. Where any imbalance manifests, be it physical or psychological, this is a result of an incorrect perception held as a deep belief somewhere in a person's memory banks [6].

There are ways to minimise a healing crisis and there is no better time to start than now. After all, there is no time like the present. As we move along this journey towards greater awareness together I hope it will become clearer, through your own insights and not just my words, just what it is that we need to do to shake off this veil that mists our perceptions.

Three

Introducing Dowsing 1: Energy Stresses

Finding the Cause of Stress

I read some years ago an article in a Newsheet published by the Dulwich Health Society number. 7, 1994 (a U.K. society dedicated to informing the public about the existence and dangers of geo-pathic stress), of case studies linking geo-pathic stress to various states of ill health. They found after having checked around 25,000 people with ill health that:

> "•100% of people who get secondary cancer are geo-pathically stressed;
> •95% of people who get cancer were sleeping and or working in a geopathically stressed place before or at the time of diagnosis;
> •96% of children who are hyperactive, have learning difficulties or are difficult to control are geopathically stressed;
> •95% of people who get AIDS are geopathically stressed;

- 80% of parents and or carers who abuse children are geopathically stressed;
- 80% of people who get divorced are geopathically stressed;
- 80% of couples who cannot have babies, one or both, are geopathically stressed;
- 80% of women who have a miscarriage are geopathically stressed;
- 80% of babies who died of cot death were geopathically stressed;
- 70% of Myalgic Encephalitis (Post Viral Fatigue) sufferers are geopathically stressed;
- 70% of people who are allergic to food/drink are geopathically stressed; and
- 95% of cows who have BSE (Mad Cow Disease) are geopathically stressed.

My own findings agree with those of the Dulwich Health Society – to a point. That point relates to those areas where distress manifests as physical, mental or emotional problems are invariably found to be geo-pathically stressed. But why should the environment in the proximity of any person or animal suffering any of the above disorders be stressed? Or is it that a major part of the planet is suffering from geo-pathic stress? The implication behind the findings, as stated above, would be that geopathic stress is a common factor in all of the above described states. Taking the corollary one step further, one could imagine that geopathic stress is the cause, or certainly a contributing factor, to any state of ill health found in people or animals living or spending time over such areas.

In some cases I am reasonably certain that geopathic stress contributes to ill health. I am also convinced that in many cases ill health contributes to geopathic stress. Take for example the recent scare in the U.K. regarding the entire cow population and Mad Cow Disease. If 95 per cent of cows with BSE are or were geopathically stressed then this would indicate that a huge proportion of the English countryside, all dairy and beef farms, were to a great extent geopathically stressed. England has its problems but I cannot reconcile these observations with my own findings. Since all life is inter-related and inter-dependant no one being can be in isolation. If you take a cow or any animal and isolate it from other members of its species or keep it in a hostile environment where the animal is unable to move around and lie in areas where it feels comfortable, you have the beginnings of a stressed cow. Anyone studying the habits of animals soon realises that certain animals enjoy the energy effects of certain areas. In many countries it is known that a cow will sleep over a 'positive' energy area. If you want to build a house and know that the energy will be good for you in that environment, simply displace the cows and put your house where they enjoyed sleeping.

To expect that animals do not suffer from stress indicates how far removed we are in our material society from understanding our natural environment. If you were to feed those cows a diet totally alien to their natural foods, one full of chemicals and hormones and even feeding the cow the offal of sheep, then is it any wonder that the cow is going to get sick? Do we blame the countryside as a contributing factor or can we face up to the reality that it is the totally un-natural treatment of the animal that has created a very stressed cow which, in turn, has created an extremely stressed environment?

Fear and Stress

If a person is suffering from severe ill health and is in a lot of pain and fear (the medical diagnosis of a terminal illness is a major stress factor in the lives of patients diagnosed with a life threatening disease) then that person will affect their total environment in an adverse way. Most people will have had some experience of taking care of a very sick or disabled person, or at least being in the company of such a person. We know on a physical, mental and emotional level the effect that such a person has on us. The closer the emotional bond, the more distress we feel. This distress and fear of seeing someone in pain who is knowingly approaching death affects us on more than a purely emotional level.

Many people have phobias such as snakes, dogs, spiders, heights, horses, open spaces and so on. Sometimes the cause of fear is quite inexplicable but the fear itself is very real to the sufferer. A story I often share in workshops centres around an early morning walk on a summer's day on Kangaroo Island in South Australia. Whilst walking barefooted over a cleared paddock one morning I came face to face with a long and poisonous King Brown snake. The snake lay in the middle of the paddock, enjoying the morning sun. I could have walked a few metres either side of the snake and been totally unaware of the snake's presence, however I seemed to head straight for it, or else the snake had placed itself right in my path. I was no more than a metre from the snake when I saw it, my foot pausing in mid stride. I must have been feeling very centred and calm that morning for I did not even flinch. I had no bodily reaction of fear or increased adrenaline or stomach tightening or fight or flight responses flashing around my mind or body.

I simply looked at the snake, and it looked at me. I apologised for disturbing the snake. We looked at each other a moment longer and then the snake slowly made its way off across the paddock and I continued my morning walk. Had I for one moment gone into fear, the snake, who is a creature that detects vibrations with its tongue, would have felt an ugly, dirty, threatening energy and would itself have felt threatened and attacked. I may not have been here to write this had I gone into fear. Simply talking about this experience sends most people into shivers of fear, but what is scaring them is a thought, nothing more. When the occasion arises we may well find ourselves dealing with a possibly dangerous situation in a calm clear-headed way. It is interesting that the thought, or a memory of all the negative outcomes of such a situation will trigger a survival response.

Thinking of a dangerous situation is enough to send some people into a fear vibration. I have spent many years blue water cruising and know how the fears that can be generated in harbour will delay or prevent a lot of people from venturing out of the safety of the harbour. Had I known I would be dealing with mountainous seas, monstrous tidal rips and fierce squalls I might never have left port myself. Not one to be daunted by what might happen, I did leave port and encountered all of the above and a whole lot more besides. As each moment presented itself, whether it be storm or calm, I needed to deal with it as it happened... and I did. The imagination creates all sorts of horrors and excuses why we cannot follow a particular path, yet when we find ourselves on that path more often than not we deal effectively with all that arises. And I still cannot swim...

Feeling Stress Energies

A snake feels vibrations and responds to them; so do we. Perhaps you have been at a party or social gathering when, upon leaving, a friend may have asked you if you saw so-and-so. No, you replied, only to discover later that this particular person was sitting nearby all evening! The energy field that we generate is read sub-consciously by all around us. If we are feeling shy, introverted or not particularly social then our personal energy field will be drawn in close to our physical form. We can then go almost unnoticed because many people rely on our energy forms to let them know we are around. Think about this for a while. At the other end of this scale, we might be inside a room with friends with our minds focussed on a discussion when a car arrives outside, a door slams and everybody in the room knows that a particular person has arrived. How is this possible? Not expecting this person to arrive, there was no fore-thought or expectancy in the minds of the others in the room. The people in the room were reading well known energy patterns, the patterns of a friend, the patterns of someone feeling very confident and outgoing. It is the memory of a feeling that alerts us to the presence of a person as a remembered energy pattern.

By suspending any judgements or preconceptions about our planet and accepting for a moment the possibility that the planet has a consciousness of its own, (as indeed all matter both sentient [feeling] and insentient [unfeeling] has), it is easy to see how any part of the whole can affect all other parts. When we live in a stressed environment, we are subtly affected by that stress in most cases. This is quite obvious as we look around at our fast paced and materially oriented western lifestyle and struggle to maintain a separate identity from all those around us. When we are stressed our total energy being radiates stress. It is like the fear/stress a snake can invoke. This stress must, by the very nature of this perception of energy, affect our total environment, not just those other people nearby but the very atmosphere of a room, even the very consciousness of the planet earth.

If we move into a stressed environment, whether that stress has been caused by natural phenomena, earthquakes, volcanic activity, geological faulting pressures or man-made disturbance, that stressed environment is going to impact upon any person that may spend time in such areas. For the moment we will deal with the physical causes for stress. Later, as we deal more and more with the part that consciousness plays in creating our reality, we can see how our very thoughts and emotions help construct life as we experience it.

Geopathic Stress

The degree to which we are affected by our environment depends upon many factors but principally upon our perception of who and what we are and how we fit into our total environment and the degrees of attachment we have to those perceptions. At this stage we will look at only those perceptions that appear as external. Our unique physiology gives us very personal reactions to various energy fields to which we are exposed. Our immune system, its strength and its ability to maintain good health plays an important part in how we react to our environment. Therefore the degree to which we are stressed by other 'external' causes will determine just how we are affected by any areas of geo-pathic stress in which we find ourselves.

By understanding areas where the earth's magnetic field is disturbed (that is geo-pathically stressed), we can see that a healthy balanced life is subjected to energy patterns that are not conducive to good health. This applies to plant life as well as to humans and animals. Many plants or types of animals find certain energy patterns more comfortable than others. Certain energy fields are detrimental to plant growth – as can be witnessed in a natural environment.

Water

Geo-pathic stress is not limited to the earth's magnetic field. Naturally occurring underground water and geological faulting pressure can also be a source of disturbing radiation. Water is quite a complex medium and many things will affect what sort of energy the water both attracts and radiates. A basic understanding of the chemistry of water helps explain how and why water behaves the way it does. Water consists of one atom of oxygen and two atoms of hydrogen. These atoms are bonded. The oxygen atom is the central atom with the two hydrogen atoms 'attached' either side. In effect this makes a triangle of three points but with no sides. Each of the hydrogen atoms 'connects' with the oxygen atom but not to each other. The angle formed by the relationship of the hydrogen atoms to the oxygen atom is called the bond angle.

The bond angle varies according to the quality or nature of the water. The more acute the bond angle, the more contaminated the water, and the more contaminated the water then the more likely that water is to collect or attract disturbed frequencies to it. If the initial water quality is good, for example, flowing naturally underground but then passing through areas of contamination, to become, say, radio-active, biologically polluted or chemically overloaded, then the quality of that water is going to be affected. The more pollution or contamination the water passes through, the more the bond angle (which simplistically can be seen to be interchangeable with the quality of the water) reduces until it reaches a point where the water is totally polluted and can absorb no more 'negative' qualities. By contrast, the more healthy the environment that the water passes through then the better the quality of that water and the greater the bond angle. As other streams mix and merge together the over-riding average bond angle will prevail, being modified by the quality of water of the other stream.

There is a direct relationship between the purity of water and consciousness. Water has been found to transmit messages, via a stream, from one person to another. Applying an understanding of the bond angle, we can see how the more acute the angle is then the more negative energy of 'consciousness' can be supported by that particular water flow. Since higher thoughts are of a higher frequency, these higher thoughts can only be attracted to and survive in water with a higher bond angle.

It follows then that water can be either beneficial or harmful depending on many factors apart from the bond angle. Flow rate, depth, the presence of other underground water courses interacting with each other and the proximity of geological fault lines also affect the type of energy generated by the water flow. For some reason certain people are strongly affected by the energies transmitted by naturally occurring underground water. Where two streams cross, particularly at different depths, energy fields have been detected which are highly disturbing to many life forms that spend time above such areas. These same disturbing frequencies can be detected where water passes through or flows within a geological fault line. Such frequencies have been found to be in the gamma range which is a highly radio-active energy that will destroy or seriously affect human cells that are exposed to such energy for any length of time.

Dowsing Water Energy

I was once asked to assist in finding a favourable location for a house and, having taken various factors into account, I advised the client accordingly. He questioned my observations and said that he would like to put his bedroom in a particular spot. When I asked, "why that particular spot?" he replied, "because I feel warm and tingly here". The warm and tingly feeling was created by an underground stream passing through a faulting pressure, thus causing a localised area of gamma radiation. I explained that this spot might be suitable for the toilet or laundry, thereby minimising exposure to it, but to put his bedroom over such an area where he would spend a considerable part of his life would expose him to stress that he could better do without. Depending on the time we spend in areas of gamma or naturally occurring micro-wave radiation or geopathic stress, also taking into account the state of our immune system and other stress factors in our lives together with the intensity of the disturbed area, physical effects such as cancer would not be an uncommon result.

If you, (or anyone you know) is restless and fitful at night and possibly has a tendency to overheat and toss the blankets off, you may well be sleeping over such an area of harmful radiation. There is enough stress in 'modern day living' without adding the burden of geo-pathic stress to our lives. A young woman complained for years of a steadily worsening pain in the shoulder. This pain developed over a long period and eventually a cancer was diagnosed. When her case was investigated, a significant area of geo-pathic stress was found in the region of the shoulder in the woman's bed. What this example illustrates is that our ability to affect our environment is a two way street. On one side is the overall physical, mental and emotional health of the person leading up to the diagnosis of any disease. On the other side we can see that certain energy patterns exist and have existed in our environment for many years.

Inherited Energies

Whenever we move into a house or build on a vacant block, the energies that are already found there are inherited energies. The energy patterns that we create are our personal responsibilities and we manage to create them wherever we go. At times we might inadvertently establish ourselves over areas of inherited energy fields that could ultimately disturb our health. No one of course would knowingly place themselves at risk. Our awareness of the impact the environment has upon us (and we on it) needs to change to enable us to make better informed decisions about where we live and work. Whilst money is worshiped to an excessive degree, issues such as fundamental cause and effect and personal health are placed on a back burner, or, even manipulated to generate more money. Treating the symptoms and not the cause is like the dog chasing its tail and just going round in circles with no real resolution in sight.

A growing awareness of our physical environment coupled with an understanding of the impact we have on that environment cannot help but lead to better health for many. Life is, after all, what we make of it.

Geo-physical disturbance is but one aspect of our total environment that we need to know more about. Such knowledge could not only improve the quality of life for all but be a foundation stone upon which we can, with the right commitment, build a sustainable future for those that follow us.

Four

Introducing Dowsing 2:
The Barriers of Technology

The side effects of 20th century technology are alarming many people and is an issue polarising the public and scientific communities. The for's and against's, always two sides, are busy building their arguments. Meanwhile the effects of this technology are like an electro-magnetic smog steadily engulfing us all. Is there any danger? Who do we believe?

Radiation: EMR and Microwave

There many factors in our modern environment that impact upon us, making it difficult to isolate 'background' effects and lay blame squarely at the feet of any one issue. With so many energy fields that are potential hazards to our well-being, everyone on the planet who takes them all seriously would be fleeing for cover – but there is nowhere to go. Not one place is safe from the monster we are creating. So, what are we to do?

In so far as the rampant growth of technology is concerned, rest assured that those responsible (be careful if you think it is nothing to do with you!) are not immune from any disturbing side effects that may surface in time.

Two specific issues are of great public concern in this period of mankind's history on planet earth. Firstly there is the Extremely Low Frequency (ELF) Electro-Magnetic Radiation (EMR) such as the electricity that powers our homes and businesses. Extremely low frequency means that the supply is at 50 cycles per second, or 50 Herz (Hz). This is a very 'un-natural' frequency and is not found in nature, certainly not in an alternating current (AC) configuration. The electrical energy field of the body, for the main part, is direct current (DC) which is a naturally occurring energy field. Our bodies resonate comfortably within this type of energy field. Alternating current (AC) is quite alien to this planet, and it has been around only for the past one hundred years or so. The other area of increasing concern is in the micro-wave band of the electro-magnetic spectrum. Figures indicate that the background levels of micro-wave radiation have increased 2 million times over the level they were 75 years ago.

Researchers into the possible effects of microwave radiation initially seemed to limit themselves to whether or not the person exposed to such energy felt warm and toasty. If not, then there was no danger. We have come a long way since then. Vested interests still struggle to maintain the illusion that these energy frequencies are not harmful. Consumer groups on the other hand struggle to present their case against dangerous levels of microwave and electro-magnetic radiation. Either way we have to survive this 'crisis'.

Until there is a dramatic shift in the collective values of humanity, the generated electrical energy that we have become so dependant upon is here to stay. Telecommunications and military use will ensure that microwave radiation levels are maintained and pushed to even greater limits.

To take a stand, wave a flag and speak up on behalf of individual causes is not my style. I believe that the more noise one makes, either for or against any point whatsoever, then the more that polarisation occurs. Polarisation can be understood as two opposing forces creating more and more tension, as the tension builds the chance of reconciliation or harmony lessens as each 'side' digs its heels in. This serves to keep the status quo and effectively ensures that any person caught up in the extreme polarity is held in separation which in turn prevents unity consciousness. However I am not sitting back and accepting all that I am told or handed. As I seek to understand the essence of who we are, polarities begin to fall away and the negative effects of any energy 'out there' have less and less impact upon me. In a word, the more we can stand in the light the less darkness there is to disturb our equilibrium. My own fear or ignorance makes me a victim of circumstance keeping me in duality. My own awakening frees me from this victim consciousness. Self-empowerment is the key. We all have the potential but what are we doing about it?

What To Do?

Firstly consider specific things such as the number and type of electrical appliances in use in the home, and perhaps computers at home and work. How often do you use a mobile telephone? Look at the position of the electrical meter box: is it near the head of your bed? High tension power lines may be having an effect upon your health: how close are they? Are you or any member of your family constantly battling ill-health? Do you receive regular medical treatment, allopathic or otherwise and show no signs of improvement?

It is possible that our homes may not be the safest places we could go to maintain good health. Looking at the possible effects of the energies contained within the earth itself we should be alerted to the fact that we, as energy bodies, depend very much on a stable, healthy energy environment. Imagine all those little cells that make up your immune system all quietly going about doing their job effectively (in a DC state) and then… Wham! You walk into a powerfully disturbing AC energy field! The cells then go into overdrive trying to maintain a balanced state. Hyperactivity, particularly in young children can be traced back to an excessive sensitivity to exposure to this type of energy. Sufferers of our 20th century syndrome who are hyper allergic to almost everything will certainly be adversely affected by extremely low frequency electro-magnetic radiation, as well as about every other petro-chemical and food additive or preservative imaginable.

Labour saving devices, which are developed around the desire to have more time available for recreation, must now be looked at more closely. Certainly they have given us more free time, but we find that the time gets taken up earning more money to support that lifestyle. The old argument that 'bigger freeways don't solve any problems, they just create bigger traffic jams applies to our obsession with time. The more time we have, the more time we seem to need. We are trapped in a circle of ever greater needs, created by our desire to have more time. Like depression though, the deeper we are in it the more difficult it is to see the way out. This might be a wonderful opportunity if you manufacture devices that save time, but these devices can also pollute the environment. The time saving slogan, together with clever advertising, blinds the consumer into buying more and more. "Find a need", say the advertisers to the manufacturers "and fill it; if you can't find a need, create one, then fill it". Our needs, it seems to me, are killing us slowly but surely. Societies that build houses without kitchens have to be viewed suspiciously, especially when in place of a kitchen we find a microwave oven, large deep freeze and a waste disposal unit. What came first – 'reality' or science fiction?

Avoiding Radiation Side Effects

If you get a headache or ringing in the ears or a tingling sensation in your arm after using your mobile phone I suggest you stop using it before you put yourself out of action. Reports indicate that a person's head can absorb as much as 60 per cent of the radiation emitted from a mobile phone. Devices have been developed and marketed in some European countries that shield the head from this radiation but the companies seem unwilling to promote such devices for fear that it may be taken as an admission that mobile phones are dangerous. American police using hand held radar guns were finding a disproportionately increased incidence of cancer of the cervix and testes in officers regularly using the radar guns. Studies in Australia have found that within four kilometres of a television tower in residential areas, rates of childhood leukemia were 60 per cent higher and mortality rates from illness were over 100 per cent higher than in another area away from the tower. This problem is not going to go away in a hurry. Reproducing these statistics is not intended to play upon the fears of anyone, rather we must become aware and move out of ignorance and fear. This I believe, will take us out of the victim consciousness, empower us to make decisions for ourselves and turn the tide of this insidious plague that threatens the continuation of life on this planet as we know it.

If you use an electric blanket and are unable to sleep, do not just turn the power off – take the plug out. Be aware also that your clock radio can generate a disturbing energy for a radius of 45 cms (18 inches). Baby alarms too have been found to have a disturbing effect within a similar range. Water beds, because of their heater, can also disturb your sleep. Remember that we go to sleep to rest and recover and build up our energies for another day. When we are under any stress whilst we sleep, we may wake up more tired than before we slept. Television sets, computers, photocopiers and other electrical items all have a mix of energy fields that affect the environment. If you feel drained and worn out at the end of a day in front of a computer, the cause may not be the workload. Certain difficulties with birth have been associated with concentrated computer use. If you are pregnant, cut down your hours at the computer and get more exercise. A negative ion generator may also prove helpful.

Some electrical appliances have a more disturbing effect on their immediate environment than others, for example hair driers and electric shavers, electric can openers, power saws, vacuum cleaners and microwave ovens. If you are concerned about breast cancer try avoiding computers and microwave ovens. Undoubtedly you will be told, depending on who you ask, that this is nonsense and that there is no evidence that these appliances affect health. Make up your own mind.

It seems unfortunate that a manufacturer can convince a government that their product is totally safe when the tests on safety have been conducted and funded by the manufacturer. Depending upon whom you talk to, microwave ovens seem to be another centre of controversy. According to the research I have read the best thing you could do with your microwave would be to take it outside and bury it if you are concerned about your family's health. Nevertheless many microwave users defend them to the last, having become totally dependant upon the time saving qualities and the reduced financial cost in cooking. Justifications abound, such as, "My lifestyle could not be maintained without it", or "I can bless or pray over my food after I have micro-waved it", or "The studies show that the vitamin and mineral content of the food has not been affected". Make up your own mind. Be open to all the arguments and decide for yourself. As we get deeper into remembering just who and what we are we become less and less concerned about microwave ovens or mobile phones. Don't despair, take a considered choice about your quality of life and stay focussed.

Living in an inescapable electro-magnetic smog does not give us a lot of room to decide on a healthy or sustainable future for ourselves. Is electro-magnetic radiation good? Is it bad? Meanwhile it just gets worse. Electro-magnetic pollution is a major factor on our planet today. It is affecting our health and the health of our children. It is one of many factors that our immune system is having to contend with. Perhaps on its own we could cope with it but in conjunction with the effects of the preservatives in our food [7], the chemicals in our water supply, the abundant use of plastics, food irradiation, the stress of maintaining a 'comfortable lifestyle' with the pressures on the family unit becoming more intense as the days go by, a healthy balance becomes harder to maintain. Crime and violence is escalating and fear of burglary, rape, mugging and worse is taking hold of people's hearts. Governments merely seek to put band aid solutions on problems they cannot deal with or even begin to see, thereby creating more tension in the population. It is no wonder that many seek salvation within religious or spiritual institutions or alien phenomena or back-to-nature scenarios.

Nevertheless electricity is here to stay, as is excessive microwave radiation and also all the rest. We have to live in the world that we have created. At this stage things get interesting (as I tell people attending my workshops) but there are a few choices. We can either resist change or suffer the consequences. We can allow our cellular structure and DNA to adjust to this new chemical and electric environment or we can die from it, as many are already.

Five

Dowsing To Discover Energies

Coming to Dowsing

We can say that whatever we do and however we change, die or evolve, these activities are all steps on an evolutionary ladder. All life is a learning and growing experience including the sickness and death parts. But who would knowingly die a painful death? My own path in my younger years was strongly influenced by my inbuilt awareness of the teachings of the Buddha. This view has expanded considerably as I have aged and gained the wisdom of those years. Some of the most exciting growth has occurred through my introduction to and exploration of dowsing, which is similar to searching for water with a divining rod but which has wider meanings apart from water. Dowsing has become an important part of my life.

There is nothing 'New Age' about dowsing. Rather, there is a growing awareness of the one-ness of all life, with dowsing happening to be a very useful tool that allows us to access information that is not openly available.

Dowsing Devices

The word 'dowsing' tends to conjure up a picture of someone walking across a paddock holding a forked stick, traditionally hazel in northern Europe and Eucalypt in Australia, searching for underground water. Some people believe that Moses used a dowsing rod to locate water in the desert. Woodcuttings from the Middle Ages depict Germans dowsing for minerals. In more recent times, dowsing was used in France to track down criminals. A Swiss dowser I know of is frequently called in by the police to help locate missing persons.

Dowsing transcends the usual channels of finding out, consequently there are many people who refuse to accept its validity. Where any person's 'comfort zone' is under threat, denial will come to the rescue. Simply because dowsing does not fit into the reality of some individuals does not mean it is nonsense.

Many books have been written on the dowsing phenomenon, with many ideas put forward to explain just how a pendulum can know the answer to a question or a dowsing rod can move when it encounters an invisible energy field. One widely accepted explanation is that the fine motor muscles in the hand are involved. The dowsing rod is a very delicate instrument and any movement of the hand or wrist will affect the movement of the rod or pendulum. Bearing this in mind it is important for the dowser not to consciously affect the pendulum or rod. This does not explain however how the dowsing can be accurate time and time again. My understanding is that by focussing on a particular question, a clear and quiet mind is as essential as is holding the right question in mind. The brain, a computer-like organ, scans the electro-magnetic spectrum in an undirected automatic way. Then it locates the particular energy 'frequency' associated with the object of the search and signals the fine motor muscles in the hand which move the rod or changes the pendulum's direction. This is a simplistic explanation but when we look at consciousness in greater detail in a later chapter it will become a little clearer to understand.

All the energy fields we have discussed are empirical, that is, they can be measured. Although the earth's magnetic field can be mapped to illustrate that the flow of the earth's energy is definitely a tangible force the equipment may not be able to distinguish between a healthy and an unhealthy energy pattern. There are devices being developed that can map underground water. Geological faults have long been able to be located and measured. The equipment needed to do this however is both expensive and time consuming. An efficient dowser can locate all of the above in a fraction of the time a machine requires, and the dowser can go into much greater detail if required.

Dowsing on Energies

Energy fields created by electrical appliances, power lines and microwave transmitters can be detected and measured. The only area of disagreement is the degree to which people can be exposed to these energy emissions. Dowsing is a very unique and personal approach to these questions. I do not ask for specific measurements of radiation, although some studies indicate certain very low levels are safe where other studies indicate much higher levels are safe. Scientists can continue this debate into the 21st century, but if I dowse for a particular person who asks if the energy from electrical or micro-wave radiation is adversely affecting this person and "yes" is the reply, then we do something about it. Why wait to be told by a government body or scientist when you know deep down inside that you are not well, and that the energy of an electrical field or micro-wave radiation is affecting you in a negative way? We do not need the proof of experts. We need to take back the responsibility for our own health and well-being.

Evidence of harmful effects continues to build up, thereby increasing public awareness and putting pressure onto manufacturers to conform to tighter standards or risk a major drop in sales. A good dowser can locate suitable boundaries of energy fields of appliances, power lines, transformers and microwave transmission towers that will be relevant to particular individuals. Each of us is different, in that we have a unique system with our own sensitivities. What is good for some may not be good for others. Knowing how close we can get to these energy fields without being adversely affected at least gives us a choice.

Dowsing can explore our physical, geo-physical and technological environment simply and quickly. The information gained can be used to create a better, healthier lifestyle.

Rods, Pendulums and Asking the Right Questions

The traditional tools of the dowser, namely a rod and a pendulum, are at once simple, inexpensive and low-tech. There are many different types of rod used, while the materials used to make a pendulum are extensive. Because it is my belief that it is not the rod or the pendulum that is doing the work, rather we ourselves, the material used is not important. The rod I currently use is a piece of stainless steel welding rod, 30 cm long. It is bent at right angles 7.5 cm from one end. I use stainless steel because it does not discolour like a coat hanger or fencing wire. Also it does not make your hand smell of metal. I choose a welding rod because it is nice and straight when you start. Straightening out coat hangers, although they are made from a soft metal, is quite time consuming if you have to make 50 or so for a workshop. I use only one rod since I find that one rod works just as well as two and it makes life easier when following the course of an underground stream or geo-magnetic field.

I have used pendulums as varied as a large nut on the end of a length of rope, a split pin on a piece of cotton, a bunch of keys, a ring on a piece of string. My preference today is a crystal on a silver chain. However anything will do because the pendulum is merely a tool that will swing freely. Although there are many different types of pendulum available, the only consistent requirement seems to be that the material is not magnetic, since many of the energies that we dowse over have a magnetic component. The reason for this becomes obvious. Specialised dowsing, such as dowsing for specific minerals, may be assisted by specific pendulums.

Holding the right question in mind is critical to the success of the dowser. When we understand that the whole of our world is energy with ever changing interfering wave patterns, then the need to be clear about what we are looking for is vital. There are many types of energy fields with many so close in frequency that an unclear question can lead to a lot of confusion. A major hurdle for inexperienced dowsers is the clarity of the question. Any ambiguity will create more confusion and the rod or pendulum will react accordingly.

Who Can Dowse?

Surprisingly, for non-dowsers anyway, studies have indicated that at least 80 per cent of the human population of the planet would have no trouble dowsing. Whether the majority go on to become highly proficient dowsers is another matter. Children make excellent dowsers due to having none of the limiting belief patterns of the adult and being more open and accepting.

When I first began to dowse I found that the rod was very responsive. This was a fortunate experience because the pendulum I was using simply refused to move and hung limply on its piece of string for three months (not that I was holding it for all that time of course). I also held deep seated beliefs about people who used pendulums, thinking them a little eccentric, even weird. So without knowing it I had set up a barrier preventing me from successfully using the pendulum. This changed as I discovered more and more 'respectable' people dowsing and was taught different techniques to access my own ability to dowse with the pendulum. Since then I have had no trouble using a pendulum. It is our own beliefs that deny us access to this wonderful little tool, and beliefs, as we will discover, are basic to all that happens to us.

Stories of dowsing abilities pop up like mushrooms. Many people will be familiar with the story of a grandmother dowsing with a wedding ring on a piece of cotton over the mother-to-be. A simple procedure to see if the child was a boy or girl. This practice is known as information dowsing, as in the case of the gardener dowsing the sex of a paw paw tree, or the farmer dowsing the sex of the eggs. Sometimes a person does not realise that he or she is 'dowsing'. People come to workshops, never having held an 'L' rod or pendulum before and within hours, to their joyful amazement, they are finding and following energy patterns. This experience is doubly rewarding when those same energy patterns are confirmed by another dowser.

Types of Dowsing

There are many stages involved in the art of dowsing and it may help to go through them as we continue to build up an overall picture of the world of energy.

On-site dowsing is the most obvious and is one of the most basic areas that needs to be mastered. On-site simply means that the dowser, armed with an 'L' rod, moves through a given area searching for a particular energy field such as water, disturbed areas etc. Upon encountering the object of the search, the 'L' rod swings to mark a boundary of the energy field, making it possible to follow that particular energy field as it flows through the environment. Depending upon the question asked, it is possible to find areas that are beneficial to human life or areas that are antagonistic. This information can be invaluable to people seeking healing areas or those being affected by disturbed energy patterns.

Horizon dowsing is a time and effort saver. Instead of wandering over a great area in search of a particular energy pattern, the dowser scans the horizon, holding an arm or some other pointer outstretched and using the pendulum in the other hand. By asking a specific question, the pendulum will indicate when the pointing arm is in line with the energy being sought.

The next stage, which may begin to defy logic, is map dowsing. Here the dowser is able to dowse over a map and ascertain a very broad range of information about the site being examined. That we can accurately assess the energy patterns in a building or on a piece of land just by dowsing over a map is quite remarkable. There are reports of the American Army using map dowsing to locate mines laid overnight by the Vietcong. The skills of detection in map dowsing are only the beginning of a much more fascinating field. The principle behind map dowsing will become clearer as we look deeper into the nature of the non-local mind.

Information dowsing is a vast field with no end to its many applications. But how can a pendulum, an inert object, advise us or supply answers to questions? What is it that is operating here? This is such a complex and involved puzzle that we almost need to know what the last piece is before we can accept the first few pieces. It seems that without solid foundations upon which to build (and in the absence of several quantum leaps in understanding and acceptance), and being locked into Earth, space and time as we are, we need to move forward slowly and gently.

Six

Learning Through Dowsing

My First Experiences

Co-operation with nature is another level of dowsing. Here we apply our understanding of the above mentioned stages and make wiser use of the energies that make up our environment.

When I first began clearing houses of stress I used various devices which shielded or altered the disturbing energy patterns in the house or workplace. I am, by nature, a little impatient and always seek to keep things as simple as possible. Whatever device I used implied that I was keeping something at bay, protecting myself from forces in the environment. I grew to be less comfortable with that concept as time went on. Not only was a considerable amount of time and effort involved, but the client came to depend upon the devices. This could be most unsettling if the devices were accidentally moved, since all the old problems would come back. I found occasionally that despite the devices the 'negative' energy patterns could return after a few weeks or so. In such cases it was necessary to look at the beliefs of the people living in the environment, keeping in mind the difference between inherited energy fields and those that we carry around with us. It was obvious that in some, if not all cases that the mind of the client either accepted the devices or rejected them, depending upon their deep seated beliefs and requirements.

This early experience prompted me to look more closely at the relationship between client and environment, a factor which has become my main focus. I find now that the same 'power' that enabled people to believe in and accept the devices applies just as strongly today in the ever more popular applications of Feng Shui in the western world.

Devices, whatever their nature, are an important part of the support system of many cultures throughout the world. We in the west, on our search for peace, happiness and wealth are now turning to the Chinese eco art of Feng Shui, hoping that answers to our problems can be found within the cultural 'devices' of another civilisation. My impatience does not allow me to rest long on my current understanding. I am forever seeking more and more fundamental reasons and explanations by driving myself into uncharted areas, often treading on thin ice, but always seeking a simpler and more fundamental solution.

Moving On

Clearly there is something deep within my very being that urges me on in my search for knowledge and wisdom. This may seem to contradict my true nature which is, for the most part, at peace with who I am, where I am and what I am.

Nevertheless I define myself as a seeker, wherever, whenever I am: it is who I am. Self acceptance is a good inner core from which to explore this universe.

Being a little discontented is always a good motivator for change, but the next and most profound change lay dormant within me, waiting its time. As I moved more and more into the dowsing work so I allowed the sleeping giant within to stir and finally awaken.

Always seeking more knowledge and wisdom and a greater understanding, I sought an astrological reading for the coming year. The astrologer confirmed the importance to me of the work I was doing. All was going well until she said, about the balance work, "And you are doing this with your mind are you?". I felt, at that point that she may have lost the plot. I strongly denied this was the case: "No", I said, "I am using these various devices". Silently we agreed not to talk about that any more and moved on. I already felt that I was on the edge of society with my beliefs and the energy dowsing. I had no intention of moving further out into the wastelands, isolating myself even further from my friends. Speaking about this to very few people, I mulled over her question for a few days then gave it no more thought.

Two weeks after the visit to the astrologer I was called in to check out the energies in a house. Synchronicity was working well since the clients had already experienced my work in their shop a month or so before. The energy levels in the shop had improved and business was going well. Since the work with the shop had been successful they decided it was time to do the house. As was my usual practice in those days I mapped out the many energy fields that were having both a positive and a negative effect on the environment and on those living in that environment.

From my feelings in the house and my analysis of the map it was clear that a lot of balancing was required. The next stage of this now outmoded process was to dowse over the energy map and find out what devices were needed to restore a balanced, harmonious energy to the home and environment. Try as I might, I could get no answers. Many breaks, cups of tea and sleeps later one question popped into my mind, "Have the changes required already happened?" "Yes", indicated the pendulum. This threw me into more confusion and many more questions. When dowsing, we have to learn to trust our intuition and have confidence in the results. Unusual answers throw the novice dowser off centre for a while and I was no exception. It was not because I did not believe that the changes could have already happened, especially recalling the words of the astrologer; it was just that I was a little slow in accepting the reality of the situation.

I began a new line of questioning which strongly indicated that when I dowsed over the disturbing energy fields in the house they had changed somehow, seemingly by themselves, into a positive, balanced state. It was early days to understand the why's and wherefore's, but change certainly seemed to have happened. I then sought answers within for the next day. I mused over a whole stream of possibilities and probabilities.

The following day I received a call from the client. She said that she was too sick to phone the day before and explained how she was feeling after my visit. Quickly I told her what I thought had happened. She seemed a perfect person to be my first 'guinea pig', and had no trouble accepting my explanation, which she said made a lot of sense. Changes for the better had occurred even though she had been expecting the physical devices.

Letting Go of Devices

Shortly after my first 'no-devices' experience, I went into the city to look at another house. The client was at home when I began mapping out the energy fields but left shortly after to go to work. Not surprisingly the very same thing happened. Arriving home I started to dowse over the energy maps to work out what devices were needed and where no devices were needed. I did not have to wait long for confirmation of the results of this job. Early that evening the phone rang. The client stated she was delighted, even though she too had expected the devices. She reported that as she unlocked the front door she felt the difference in the energy of the house. "Lighter", "happier", "more positive" were only some of the words used. Obviously something was happening, something quite profound, as I innocently moved through a house dowsing. That was many years ago and, needless to say, I do not use devices anymore.

As a result of this revelation and many hours of dowsing and practical hands-on experience, coupled with extensive anecdotal feedback from satisfied clients, I realised that it was solely my intent, as I made the device, that changed the energy in the environment. My intent was to restore harmony and balance to the environment and this intent met the particular requirements of those living in the house, not my own perceptions of what is right or wrong. I studied this phenomena carefully before 'going public'.

It seemed that the device merely anchored the intent and gave the client a point of focus for the changes. On another level this could apply to the traditional cures used in Feng Shui: firstly a commitment to change is required, then a request for a practitioner for whom you have high regard to come in and – voila! the disturbance is cleared. There are many people who require obvious evidence of change or work done and there are people available to meet those demands. More and more however I find people wanting to accept greater responsibility for their own lives and, once things are explained to them in terms they can readily understand, they are only too willing to accept their part in the creation of their own reality.

Bridging the Material and Spiritual

Dowsing is not only a simple tool to explore our unseen universe, but more importantly it is a tool for personal growth. It is like a bridge between the known or easily accessed information and the hidden or esoteric knowledge. When people explore the material world and reject the spiritual, their natural sensitivity to the total environment seems to atrophy. They might justify this rejection by saying that have been dragged into materialism or any other 'ism. They might also say that people have been denied spirituality by the priesthood and have been guided into a patriarchy that they did not want. But if we find ourselves blaming the past or others for the ills and predicaments in our life, then we are, subconsciously, maintaining a polarity between our perceptions of good and evil. By maintaining that polarity or duality we can never experience the one-ness, the unity of all beings. This may not be your personal goal right now, however it is important to realise that the duality or polarity that we support by our personal beliefs is that force which creates our good or bad experiences in life.

Learning Through Dowsing

Whatever our focus may be, dowsing is like a key to a door that has been locked for a long time. We are incredibly sensitive beings but that sensitivity to our total environment has been suppressed in low frequency needs and desires. Whilst we are kept in a subtle but constant state of anxiety merely to survive in a material world we have little time available for reflecting and questioning the reality of that situation. becomes swamped and we begin to lose touch with who we are. This collective 'victim consciousness' allows those that seek power at any cost to more easily control and manipulate a consumer market, thereby increasing their own power and control.

It is as if we have all become controlled by the activities of the 'left brain' – the intellectual side – at the expense of the more balanced outlook combining the 'right brain' or instinctual processes. Art has been a tolerated release over the centuries but spirituality has not. Art must comply with the social standards of the day, to a point. Much 'art' is progressive, whether it be music, painting, sculpture or the performing arts but art is born within certain social conditions. Humankind has sought to express its higher, more spiritual nature through art since time immemorial. For those that were already in touch with the higher nature of the self, persecution, torture and death were the likely outcomes. This applied primarily in the western cultures and patriarchal societies, but anywhere a priesthood then grew a hierarchy of control developed. The instinctual side of our nature was gradually 'taken away' from us. Our personal powers were usurped with that old promise of "it is for your own good", which of course means it is in the priesthood's best interests.

If we cannot get back in touch with our 'right brain' instinctual abilities we tend to miss the obvious. Dowsing helps (in a left brain way) to open us up to our feelings. This is a very difficult process for a culture that basically denies it has feelings. If we could truly feel our environment and not just pay lip service to it then we would never treat it as we do, nor allow anyone else to treat it with such disrespect. Whilst we cannot feel the environment, or feel (know) the consciousness of the earth, in our ignorance we justify our actions with the political and social calls for progress. For me at least, dowsing gives access to the world of feeling and sensitivity that is beginning to open up a wondrous world where anything in possible.

Advice for Beginners

As I continue to use the 'L' rod and pendulum to enter this world of energy awareness I 'need' the tools less and less. There are many people who do not need any tools, having the confidence and awareness to ask the right questions. But for the majority of people, dowsing is a convenient way to begin that journey. One of the good things about dowsing is that when you are finished, you can 'turn off' and have a rest, all the time building up your system to cope better with the increased sensitivity that you are feeling.

It has been said that dowsers are noted for dying while still quite young. I have not managed to scare anybody away from workshops with that statement but it is interesting to try and understand why that should be so. I believe that as we dowse we scan the spectrum of energies seeking out a particular frequency. Dowsing has been likened to a meditative state in which a dowser's brain wave patterns move into the same frequencies as those found in people who meditate – but with one difference. The dowser has awakened the part of the brain that enables him or her to scan the electro-magnetic spectrum whilst remaining in a meditative state. Holding this quiet state amid the bustle of life around them is a problem for beginners and leads to confused answers and incorrect diagnosis. Whilst remaining very still and focussed in the mind, the brain is searching out various energy patterns looking for the frequency that matches the question.

When I first started dowsing, several energy fields that I encountered had a draining effect on my own energy. Amongst these were electro-magnetic radiation from high tension power lines or transformers and microwave radiation. These are not the only energy patterns that can affect us in such a way, but the process of development that makes a good dowser is a slow, personal journey. We only seem to encounter energies that we are capable of dealing with or that will stretch us a little. This is a safety valve that ensures we will not die too young. For many dowsers who operate knowingly or unknowingly on the levels we have already discussed, namely on-site, horizon, map, information and co-operation with nature, they are exposing themselves to an incredible array of energy patterns that they would normally have shielded out. This shielding can be seen as a lack of sensitivity to our environment or a deliberate process whereby we have closed down certain centres, thinking them to be evil or harmful.

It is the very nature of dowsing to open and and seek out. It is a lack of sensitivity to our natural environment that is the issue here. By denying this connection with our natural world we unknowingly put up barriers to protect ourselves from the dangers of the natural world. This barrier-raising has not happened overnight, and aside from superstition, would not have been developed on purpose. These barriers are what keep us from understanding more about our world and our place in it, – but at the same time putting us in a catch 22 situation: the barriers appear necessary to protect us; at the same time it is the barriers that prevent us from realising our true natures and the freedom that awareness brings. At first glance this explanation may appear to be a nasty conundrum with no way out other than a great leap of faith. Faith might help, but dowsing is gentler and will lead you to the point where a leap of faith is no big deal.

So why do dowsers die young? Opening ourselves up to energy fields that have long been denied by the conscious mind exposes the body to all sorts of energies to which it is not accustomed. If we fail to realise what is going on, for example why we feel tired and drained after a job and what needs to be done to correct the situation, then we put our immune system under incredible stress. Naturally the immune system can only take so much before starting to malfunction. It is a resistance to change that ultimately affects us and causes sickness, disease and death. The death of the physical however is not the end that many believe. Death cannot automatically bestow peace and happiness, oneness or nothingness.

Exploring Memory and Consciousness

The reason why some people resist change more than others is due to an addiction to certain memories. Interesting and unpleasant experiments on rats to try and locate where memory was stored produced some interesting findings. After removing a part of the brain, turning it around, even mincing it and putting it back, scientists found that memory was not affected. They then concluded that memory was not stored in the brain. Using the concept of the holographic universe and applying it to individual manifestation within the holograph, some scientists believe they have found the answer to understanding memory. Not only did the holographic principle explain memory but a lot more psychic phenomena as well. Memory is accessed by the brain but not stored in it.

Looking at this concept another way, it is as though we are swimming in a collective cosmic sea of consciousness. In this sea there is no point where one being ends and another begins. This sea could be called divine consciousness, the Akashic records or, as I call it, non-local mind. Since all parts of a hologram – or in the case of this highly complex ever changing manifestation that we call life, the "holoverse" – contain the information for the whole, then we are able to act like personal transceivers, namely receiving information from our total environment via the physical and subtle bodies, translating it into useable energy via the chakra system and transmitting energy via our thoughts, words and emotions. It becomes easier to see just how powerful an impact we have on our total environment when we view things this way. This sea of consciousness is a cosmic soup as it were, containing the total information of everything past, present and future. The 'soup' is consciousness and as such is beyond time and space. Because we have taken on a physical form, we have entered into a physical world where time and space are basic limiting factors to our overall experience. Consciousness however is not limited to time and space.

Communication and the 'Web of Indra'

Quite recently the technology to take measurements faster than the speed of light became available to scientists. One of the experiments, Bell's Theorum (named after Alexander Bell) entailed splitting a photon (a particle of light) and moving the two particles in different directions. One photon's path was then altered and by using an extremely sensitive measuring device it was found that the instant the particle altered course, its partner also changed course, maintaining the same co-relation to its other half. This interaction happened faster than the speed of light, an event that either contradicts Einstein's theory of relativity or indicated something else was happening. It was indeed something else. Scientists came to the conclusion that the particles were never separate in the first place. Communication was instant, as it is in a hologram, where each part has the information of the whole. The soup itself was merely the medium through which the information was transferred.

The Hindus had a simpler way of explaining this phenomenon many hundred of years before Einstein or Bell were born. They called this the "Web of Indra", imagining all life interconnected by threads of energy to form a fourth dimensional web. At the point where one thread crosses another lies a pearl which is the consciousness of a human being. All the pearls are connected to each other by the web. A candle is then lit and the light shines on a pearl. The instant this pearl is illuminated all the other pearls glow. This implies that on one level we are all aware of everything that is happening throughout the universe all of the time. Such a concept is difficult to accept at first, and perhaps even more so as we consciously barely know who we are let alone what makes the universe tick. As we explore this idea further perhaps it becomes less 'crazy'. There are many reasons why we do not have access to all the information in the universe all at once. One reason is that our minds would not be able to cope, (for 'minds' read 'personal, ego based minds' not 'non-local mind'). According to Buddhist tradition it is our karma and obscurations that prevent us from accessing this information. To be in a state where we are always receptive to this energy would, according to Buddhists, be Nirvana (enlightenment), a state of bliss where everything just is. A state of omnipotence, omnipresence and omniscience (being all powerful, all present, all knowing) is constantly available within the holoverse.

As physical beings and manifestations of the holoverse we appear in the explicate order of life. On the other side of the coin, the un-manifest or implicate order is the body of the soup from which all life manifests. This physical reality is, in some ways, a projection of consciousness from within the implicate order of the universe. Without having the consciousness in the implicate order we could not exist as physical beings in the explicate order. As within, so without.

Seven

Understanding Memory

DNA As One Source Of Memory

Our current reality is based on memories that we have stored of past events. Memory itself can be genetic memory, stored in our DNA. This 'memory' also called biological memory has been handed down by our parents and their parents and forebears. What we think is what we are and our thoughts are based on our memories. Through our fundamental genetic coding we are given a building base for experience, upon which we see life and record our experiences as memory. This original coding that we 'came in with' will have a major bearing on how and what experiences we attract to ourselves and how we will react to them. We have the memory of the physical-ness of our nature; we have the memory of the soul's experiences; and we have the progressive build up of memories seen and experienced through this physical, emotional, mental and spiritual body.

Our DNA can be likened to a computer chip (a few years ago it would have been likened to a whole library of books). Understanding how so much information can be stored on such a small object as a micro-chip, we can see more easily how the DNA can hold such a vast amount of information. Our physical-ness is contained within the DNA in the same way as the carrot is contained within the seed. Height, weight, colour of hair, eyes and skin are genetic in origin. Organs, muscles and skeleton, though unique to the individual, are also genetic. This DNA package of information which takes on the form of a human being has evolved over millennia and is handed down through the generations. However it is not the only way we gather memory. As we grow we are conditioned by our social environment. Our parents, siblings, socio-groupings, economic factors, religious affiliations, political considerations all contribute. We never stop experiencing life and therefore gathering memories.

A Morphogenetic Source

There is a further way of accessing memory, that is, collective memory, directly through the soup. Rupert Sheldrake proposed the concept of the morphogenetic field whereby species were able to share personal experiences and add them to the consciousness of the whole. This 'added sharing' made those experiences available to the species via consciousness and not biological memory. It is information added to the soup by individuals, a type of cosmic internet where information once realised is made available to all.

By looking at a particular species there is plenty of evidence to support the morphogenetic field idea. One example is the hundredth monkey syndrome. On an island off the coast of Japan (if I remember correctly), a group of monkeys were very partial to the local sweet potato. Unfortunately it grew in the sand which was very gritty between the teeth when eaten. The monkeys learnt to overcome this problem by taking the potato to the beach and washing it in the sea. Soon monkeys on other islands scattered across the planet were seen to be doing the same thing. Up to the time that the first monkeys had started washing their potatoes none of the other groups were seen to wash their food.

In the United States an experiment working with rats on learning times for specific tasks found that a group of rats took six weeks to learn a specific task. Using other rats the same experiment was carried out in the U.K. The new rats took just four days to learn the same task. Mice coming into a laboratory where experiments had been done on other mice were seen to become very agitated as they picked up on the 'feeling' in the laboratory left by the previous mice who had suffered. Evolution of a species takes a new turn when morphogenesis is accepted as a factor.

Returning then to memories that we learn through our own life experiences, we can see that some good and some not so good events in our past have shaped our lives. The fundamental coding in the DNA gives a foundation upon which we add our own experiences. If we try to work out where all this started we are doomed to failure. The memories themselves are the only clues we have and the answer lies beyond the memories: another catch 22 situation. It seems to me that most problems in the world today (if we can grace the apparent chaos and confusion with the term "problems"), arise because we rely solely on old memory patterns to define our reality. Our inflexibility is holding us to a self destructive pattern like an addiction to a video, playing the same movie over and over again.

John Bradshaw, a famous American family psychologist commented that it is not so much the trauma that creates dysfunction or disturbance in our lives, it is the inability or lack of opportunity to talk about the trauma that weighs so heavily upon us. A traumatic event, for example, might be buried deep down if a person is ashamed of it or at least of its revelation to others. This is a powerful memory that will seriously affect the functioning of the individual all through his or her life if something is not done to release the tension around that memory.

Sourcing our Memories

Memory recall is not to be found in any one specific location, certainly not in the brain alone since the whole body is a complex arrangement of multiple frequencies. An interesting fact about frequencies is that each vibration or frequency has a particular colour representing it. Each frequency also has a sound or harmonic associated with it. An emotion, for example, has a particular frequency. Anger and love can be differentiated by their frequencies. Various muscle groups operate within certain frequency ranges. Energy, as memory and as frequency, can be stored in various groups of muscle as tension. Some healing modalities such as massage, reflexology, pressure point therapy, acupressure and acupuncture focus primarily on releasing energy blocks at points where tension builds up. Some readers may have experienced an emotional release or healing crisis after certain muscle groups have been stimulated. This is because those muscles held tension, that is, memory of trauma.

Memory is a very personal and intangible thing. We assume that memory is stored in some physical yet somehow nebulous part of our anatomy. Our limiting concepts of self impose limitations on just how and where that memory is stored. In order to more fully realise our potential we need to break out of the limiting perceptions of self to really understand what this thing called 'memory' is and how it is running our lives.

There is however more than one way to release old memory patterns. A wonderful story illustrating the power of cellular memory was told by Dr. Deepak Chopra about a woman having a heart transplant. When a suitable heart became available, surgery went ahead with no further delays. The woman awoke from the anaesthetic with a most unusual craving for a beer and some chicken McNuggets, neither of which she liked. A day or two later she had a dream in which a person named Dave told her how much he loved her because she had Dave's heart. The woman felt most unsettled. The next day the woman checked out the obituary notices and newspaper items around the time she had the operation. There it was: Dave, drunk at the time, had died in a motorcycle accident whilst coming out of a McDonalds take-away. A coincidence? Hardly. The memories, or the 'imprint' of Dave's consciousness was still strong in the cells of the heart. Over time (because the body is constantly replacing and rebuilding itself) the consciousness of the recipient of the heart would take over and the cells containing Dave's memories would be lost. This would be expected as long as there was no connection maintaining the programming, as in this case of the heart to its original owner, Dave.

Such an experience could put recipients of organs into a dilemma, especially in cases where organs are taken from baboons or hearts from pigs whose DNA has been manipulated to lessen the chance of rejection. With this information we can no longer see the organ as a 'spare part' but rather as a living, conscious, part of another species with the genetic and cellular memory of that species. This should make us think at least twice before accepting such an organ.

The Role of Stimuli in Sourcing Memories

It is through the connection of consciousness and memory that the integrity of the cellular memory is maintained thereby connecting the artifacts to their maker. When the connection is severed, in this instance when no more energy is supplied in the form of belief, then an opportunity to change the memory may exist. Traditional cultures here in Australia, (as elsewhere) maintain their tribal histories and a connection to their mythology through the belief patterns of each tribe. Consequently the memory of the mythology is kept alive as long as the various cultures within it continue to believe in and support their tribal mythology. If sufficient people subscribe to a perception of reality, be it a creation myth or otherwise, the 'energy' around the myth becomes an integral part of the reality of the culture. This belief can be so strong that the memory of the myth becomes itself a reality.

This connection applies to just about every institution in the Western culture as well. Any social organisation is but a collective belief. Whether it be social order, the church, the banking or legal systems, each organisation depends on the belief, continued goodwill and active support of its followers to maintain its integrity. If people across the planet were to stop believing in the Catholic Church or capitalism, the whole structure would collapse, as has happened in the so-called 'Communist' countries of Russia and Eastern Europe. So it is with governments. Generally a change of government is achieved through a vote or rebellion: people withdraw support from one person or party and transfer their allegiance to another.

What we are dealing with here is a much more fundamental level of change. We are not trying to change the existing order by revolt; instead we seek to change from within by changing our attachment to our memories. We do not want to destroy our memories because they are a fundamental reason for our being. What we need to change is how we perceive our memories.

We all have particular emotional responses to certain stimuli. The emotional response to a certain situation in one culture may be basically different to that experienced by another culture. Wars arise, for example, when one group feels it is right and tries to impose its perception on another group. If one wants change and the other resists change, then the result is invariably conflict. This does not only happen on a national scale, it is happening all the time within us. One part of us, whether it be the mind, the heart, the spirit or the body, is in conflict with another part to the degree we live in separation. Whilst we have this internal conflict within it is hardly surprising that there is so much conflict manifesting in the external physical world.

What would happen if we all withdrew our support of violent conflict and unethical behaviour? This is a dream of course, for there is always some group somewhere ready to take advantage of weakness. What would happen too were we to realise that each of us is omnipotent, omnipresent, omniscient? Consider the saying attributed to Jesus Christ: "All this and more shall you do." To whom was he talking? Did he just make it up? If we could only realise that we are working miracles every day! It is in the natural order of the universe that we work these 'miracles'. Unfortunately our creative abilities are so suppressed, so hidden, that we have forgotten they are there and that they have always been there. Our attempts at creation now are puny when they are based on our greed, the perceived wants of the body, power, glory, control, or protection from our own darker side that is sometimes referred to as the collective shadow. As long as we maintain this particular reality there is no possibility of our creative powers shining through and liberating us from our own darkness.

Our memories control our future; or to be more precise, our attachment to (or revulsion of) our memories creates our future.

To help loosen the hold our memories have over us it is important explore what consciousness is and how consciousness is going to help us.

Eight

Understanding Consciousness

Where to Start

We have already put our little toe into the cosmic soup, testing to find out if there are any piranhas in the soup. Unfortunately there are piranhas there and plenty of sharks too, but there are also dolphins and unicorns, ghouls and gremlins, fairies and angels. The soup is, after all, everything that we and every other being on this planet can possibly imagine and a whole lot more.

There is an abundance of literature today which details out of body experiences and near death experiences (NDE) as well as easy to understand books on the Buddhist and Christian interpretations of consciousness, or the essence that is behind all manifestation of life. The more esoteric teachings of the life of Christ, the hidden works, are not so different from Buddhist or ancient Egyptian or any major religion or philosophy. Each has its own slant on how things are and how they have been affected by time and translation, political expediency or spiritual power plays, but the essence of each is similar. Many people will disagree with the ideas expressed in these books, some violently as their attachment to their memories kicks in and fires them up to attack any views other than their own. It is this attachment to how things are or should be that dictates an individual's reality. Perhaps if everyone were to believe in the same thing then it would all work out fine. Think back to those that have tried to force that situation on others, not so many years ago.

The Consciousness of Energy

By looking at some of the more metaphysical reasons for disturbing energies in our environment we get a deeper understanding of the nature of consciousness. It is always important to remember that it is our perception and our reaction to energy feelings that dictates a positive or negative response. Energy itself is quite neutral. Certainly if we try to understand what energy is – and what we are – we will realise that it is our memories of past events that have built up a particular response pattern to our current experiences. This realisation will give us room to manouver or to take a step back and observe how we are responsible for particular emotional reactions. If we never take the opportunity to observe our 'selves' then we are spending all of our time here on this planet in a deep victim consciousness, which only serves to maintain duality or separation.

When I am called in to check the energy fields in a house or business I find, more often than not, that one of the basic causes for any disturbing effects being experienced is an occupant's unique response to the energies in the environment. In order for a person to react to an environment there must be something happening in that environment to triggers such as a response. Frequently we react to energies that have been left behind by previous owner/occupiers or someone with attachment to the land or building or to any object in the building or any 'trauma' that the consciousness of the land has experienced.

Only by accepting the concept of non-local mind can we see that everything is energy and that on one level or another all energy has some degree of consciousness. Thought is energy because thoughts have frequencies. Emotions are energy and are more obvious than thoughts; different emotions having different frequencies. Fear is a background energy for many, with a low, heavy sort of frequency. At least that may be how it is interpreted. Like the snake which picks up energy patterns, vibrations or frequencies with its tongue and responds immediately to those frequencies it recognises as threatening, fear has its own frequencies which the snake recognises and interprets as danger, causing it to attack.

Emotions and Energy

Another example of the fear vibration occurred at a house occupied by a single mother and her daughter. Their great dane paced the verandah trying to get into the house when I was there. To the amazement of the daughter the dog had not barked at me. I was told the dog had a habit of breaking in and tearing men's arms off!...The dog finally broke into the house and pinned me up against the wall where it proceeded to lick me unmercifully, to the great surprise of the owners. Animals do not have the number of layers of conditioning or social niceties, (even the need to not be rejected by being honest) that many humans have. They recognise friend and foe through their understanding and interpretation of energy patterns. Any energy pattern that an animal associates with ill treatment will be met accordingly. In my case, with the great dane, the dog did not feel any fear emanating from me, nor did it experience anger or aggression. Instead it felt a powerful, positive energy glow to which it was instantly attracted. It is primarily the absence of fear that is required to allow us to communicate on this level with animals.

Energy Radiations ('Vibes')

Of course we humans are a part of this interaction of energy patterns too. We may feel attracted to someone or even repulsed by a person for inexplicable reasons. We pick up on the energy of the person and that energy resonates with certain patterns we hold in our own energy field, some of which we are comfortable with and others we do not like. In the 1960s it was called the vibes. It is still the same energy but known by many other names now. We have many ways of recognising other energies. Our preoccupation with material wealth and addiction to the pursuit of happiness has closed us off from many of the senses available to us and we fail to recognise what is happening and why.

We are continually radiating energy patterns of who we are, how we feel and what we think. These energy patterns are read in many ways: visually (the most obvious); aurally; even by smell and touch. Yet there is something else that is not so obvious, namely, as we broadcast who we are, so are we able to receive that same information from others. This is commonly referred to as the 'sixth' sense. We all have this sixth sense ability which in some people is more refined and obvious than in others, but is there none-the-less. It is one of the special ways we have of recognising others: from their unique energy pattern.

By developing and using this sixth sense we learn to respect it. Dowsing is a wonderful key to greater knowledge of this ability. As we access this sixth sense more and more and learn to trust it, either through anecdotal feedback or judging it by results, a whole new world opens up to us. It is through this ability that I have come to learn about a world that is beyond the five senses, yet one that is frequently scorned as nonsense by many who have not opened themselves to this natural ability. Metaphysical energies contain, amongst other things, the very secrets of our being. Knowing this makes this journey so exciting. Not only are we able to access information from these energies that expands our understanding of life, but this awareness brings liberation.

'Seeing' Matter and Non-Matter

David Ash, a physicist, expanded on the work of Scottish scientist Lord Kelvin by proposing that the very basis for all life is the vortex [8]. According to Ash, atoms and sub-atomic particles have a unique rate of spin. An interesting observation is that energies with a rate of spin within certain parameters can only 'see' energies with a similar or lower rate of spin. We commonly accept that we are living in a three dimensional world (3D). This means that our perceived reality has time, space and depth, we can 'see' energies that spin at a particular rate or even below that rate. The Earth appears solid because the matter that makes up the physical earth is vibrating at a relatively low rate, certainly well within the parameters for us to see and experience it. Plant life, that is, the physical manifestation of plants, vibrates within our observable parameters. The slower the vibration the more solid the object: hence our physical body takes on the total appearance of being solid. According to the holographic, or more accurately, the holoverse view of life, all matter manifesting in the physical (explicate) order has a higher energy form in the that order. We could call this higher energy form our 'soul', possibly our higher self which is beyond time and space.

We see matter and recognise it as solid because of its frequency patterns. Because we cannot see matter does not imply that it does not exist. We cannot see magnetic fields or see electrical fields or microwave or gamma radiation, yet they exist. Before the technology was available for measuring these energies, anyone proposing their existence had a difficult time proving it, just as the flat earth theory was around for a very long time before it was dislodged from popular thinking. If we deny an energy exists simply because technology has no way of measuring it, we are only setting ourselves up for some embarrassment at a later date and will need to rethink or retract statements made at the time of our limited awareness. For many people however, such limited beliefs cannot be retracted and must be defended, although as time moves on their arguments become more untenable and the polarity established by holding and defending such positions creates unbearable conflict. When we look at personal health we find the same 'conflict of interests' and the tension created by it is the likely basis for all sickness.

Opening Up the Way We See

We need to open ourselves to the possibility that there are other energy patterns that we have not yet begun to recognise. Scientists eventually find what they are looking for by setting an experiment to prove an hypothesis. Without some preconception of what it is you are looking for it is very difficult to find anything or to know it when you have found it. So it is with the more metaphysical energy patterns. If you do not believe in their existence you will find it difficult to observe them. Likewise if you have an open and enquiring mind, the universe will unfold its full glory. You may be the only person to witness it in your own unique way, in which case you may find yourself in a lot of trouble convincing others of the reality of your experience. Public acceptance aside, as you access certain energy patterns you make them more available to others even though you may not be aware of this. Whether or not others can see the universe and all its glory, in the same way as you, depends on the memory patterns that limit or comprise each individual.

The reason for this explanation about energies is that we need to realise that we see life through a very narrow slit, something akin to Ned Kelly's helmet or the armoured helmets of medieval knights. The narrow slit through which we view life, which in turn is the basis upon which we judge ourselves, others and our environment is the limit we impose upon ourself. Limitations of time and space and the limits of the nervous system of the human form are inherently a part of our being since they are the medium through which we observe and acquire experience. But by acknowledging consciousness as the life beyond the form, then it is evident that this 'consciousness' must have chosen this form and must have knowingly accepted the limitations of that form. In this sense it can be said that this is a self imposed limitation. If we are able to widen the slit and observe life without such restrictive limitations we will be able to comprehend a greater reality. This reality has always existed and always will exist. It has always been available to us had we been willing to look in the right direction and ask the right questions. The Buddhist Nirvana is attainable here and now, not something that we have to wait for, or even work toward. Recognition of it is sufficient. Recognition is in the here and now, not as the result of an incredibly long and drawn out process. The Buddhists believe that it is our karma [9] and our obscurations (limiting belief patterns and the like) that prevent us from realising Nirvana here and now. This belief can lead us into a process of healing karmic patterns and releasing and moving beyond limiting beliefs. I call this process 'Life'. As we shall see, life in itself limits us [10]. If we could but see it, we are already in heaven or hell.

Is Belief the Same as Knowledge?

As mentioned previously, if we were to access the secrets of the glory of the universe, our simply accessing this knowledge would make it easier for the next person [11].

The more people subscribing or having access to certain information the more 'real' or 'solid' that information becomes and the easier it is for others to access it. What seems to happen is that many people think that having moved beyond the constraints of the physical they have discovered the 'secrets' of the universe. At this point we need to spend some time looking at consciousness as an unbroken thread in order to better understand this process.

To believe that this physical life is "it" – nothing before and nothing after – could lead to a nasty surprise. Many people do believe this however and will strongly defend that belief, although this does not mean that they are in any way brighter, sillier or wiser than anyone else. Nor does it mean that they are more (or less) evolved. An attitude is merely an attitude after all. Yet we are all a finger snap away from complete understanding and re-unification with the one-ness of all life. Some seem to choose the long way round; some become so addicted to life in three dimensional space time they cannot or will not accept liberation.

If, however, you have a nagging doubt at the back of your mind that something exists beyond the death of the physical then this point of view will be so much easier to accept. You are not neccesarily more (or less) evolved than any other being manifesting on this planet but have chosen to open yourself to the possibility that life means a lot more than living three score years and ten. If you do not ask the right questions you will not get the right answers.

The notion of a free will, co-creative planet is that whatever we apply ourselves to sooner or later manifests in the physical. (Free will is seemingly abused by many, either through design or ignorance). I read somewhere,"You cannot possibly imagine what you have not experienced." If we look at that idea closely and not just accept (or dismiss) it we could learn a lot about ourselves. What does it mean "You cannot possibly imagine what you have not experienced"?

The Non-Local Mind

'Non local mind' is the consciousness that is beyond the physical form. It is able to observe the dying or dead physical form and return to a 'living' state to describe details that are impossible to have been gathered by ordinary consciousness. Out-of-body and near-death-experiencers all point to something other than the physical, to something that continues to register experiences after the physical body has died.

Personally I think that a lot of near death experiences are too short to give us any real information. According to Tibetan Buddhist texts, the bright light that is observed at the moment of death is the dawning of the ground luminosity and is the true nature of mind. These insights should not be seen as limited to Tibetan culture but they apply equally to each one of us. They state that the dawning of the ground luminosity is just the beginning of the journey of the consciousness after physical death, and, as the path unfolds, various stages of awareness surface, eventually leading to rebirth in the physical realm. This is not necessarily how it has to be since the journey depends greatly on the level of awareness and attachments the person had prior to death. For a well trained or aware soul, remaining in the light is the end of the journey. Most people returning to 'life' from the near death experience have only glimpsed the realisation of the true nature of mind and have not yet begun the next stage of the journey. It is reported that, after having left behind the 'true nature of mind', it is very difficult to return to the physical body and full physical consciousness. Stories that we hear reported by those that have experienced the near death state are full of light and hope but tend to be misleading, since they have not continued along the whole way and experienced their personal 'dark sides'. We are led to believe that is it all love and light at the end of the tunnel because no one has returned from a more complete exploration of the experience.

The Buddha was reported as saying that we have been everyone's mother, father, son and daughter. We need not take that literally, but through the unity of consciousness (the oneness of all life, the cosmic soup or the non-local mind) we indeed have been all of those people, and more, much more. As a physical being and personality with no understanding of life beyond death, we limit ourselves and from this limitation cannot even entertain the idea of being everybody's 'mother'. From a unity of consciousness viewpoint however, it could be no other way. It seems to me that we must have signed some official secrets act before taking birth in a 3D world promising not to remember everything. If we did remember everything there would be little point in taking birth here because it would give us an unfair advantage over every other being on the planet. Rather we re-awaken gradually, possibly collectively. This way, with growing self awareness and self responsibility, we are less likely to abuse our fellow creatures. This is unfortunately not guaranteed, but, after all, there is freedom of choice.

A Personal View of Channelling

Many examples and stories of out of body experiences are already in print so it is not my intention to prove this reality but to explain it in a way that may not have been looked at before.

"Channelling" seems to have become a popular parlour game amongst some seekers, that is, those people who think there is something to look for and that the answers are to be found 'outside'. Guidance can be found yet confusion abounds – the truth is available and always has been for those that know where to look. We are not islands, not separate, isolated individuals lost in some cosmic joke. As we near the truth it becomes less frightening, less threatening to a person who has doggedly held on to its identity for so long. We are all pieces of the greater puzzle or hologram. The less fear we carry with us the higher energy state or vibration we are able to maintain. The higher the vibration, the less fear can remain in our total energy fields. The less fear, the more love: which is the secret in a nutshell. Love is the magic word, the all powerful mantra that, once ignited, will drive out the demons of greed, fear and ignorance forever. Not passionate love, not lust, not dependency, not 'my cosmic partner' but total, unconditional, non-judgmental love.

One of the interesting aspects of the rapid growth of channelling is the source of the channelled information. As Stuart Wilde once said of someone's uncle Fred: "If you are as thick as two planks when you are alive, you are as thick as two planks when you are dead". We need to be able to discern the source of any channelled information.

Differentiating Vibrations

By understanding all matter as energy that vibrates at different frequencies and by combining the vortex theory, thus assuming that we can only see that which vibrates at a similar or lower level to our own abilities, we have to deal with the fact that energies which vibrate at a higher frequency to our patterns can see us but we, who vibrate at a lower frequency, cannot see them. Through personal experience this has become quite obvious to me. If you have not experienced this (and think it a little crazy) I would certainly have agreed with you a few years ago.

There is a rapidly growing awareness and a greater degree of sensitivity as more and more people are beginning to open up to aspects of themselves that they had strongly denied. As we tune in to higher energies and collectively raise our frequencies, the gap closes between the manifest, physical energy forms and the metaphysical or spiritual energies. Our increasing sensitivity allows us greater awareness of the 'beyond'. More and more reports of near death experiences support the idea that something (we do not quite know what) lives on after death. This awareness brings its own problems, very much related to the personal consciousness of the individual. Entities wanting to jump on the band wagon abound. Any spirit or consciousness that has unmet physical desires, whether it encourages addictive behaviour or not, seeks to express its own views through an active ego or is truly able to help with valuable information.

Accessing higher energies can be likened to listening to the radio. A young child turning the radio on plays with the tuner and scans a broad range of transmissions. Because the child has not learnt to differentiate between stations there is no selective listening. The child may naturally prefer a particular station. Music would likely draw its attention but it does not know where the music is coming from or how it gets into the radio, along with all the other 'noises', or even who is singing the song. The child is scanning a broad range of frequencies, picking up different transmissions. This is how channelling operates. By scanning, or making yourself available by tuning in to a particular frequency, the channel plucks information out of the airwaves of the cosmic soup.

Simply because we open ourselves to higher frequencies of information does not necessarily mean that the information will come from a wise source. The vortex concept which states that energies of a higher frequency can see those of similar or lower frequencies applies here as well. Because energy, in this case in the form of information, comes from the 'beyond', does not mean it comes from a reliable source. By an increasing rate of spin the higher vibrational energies do not take a quantum leap from our reality and end up bundled in another higher pattern; rather they are graded, much like the rainbow. From black to white there are an infinite number of greys. Naturally the higher up the scale you go the clearer and more reliable the information you receive.

In order to tune into the higher frequencies you need the equipment to do the job. We have the equipment, that is not a problem, but fine tuning a nervous system is another matter altogether. If you put two thousand volts of electricity through a television set it would simply explode. If you try to put too much power through a human nervous system it will break down (or more likely it will not work since self-preservation would prevent you accessing higher levels of energy than you are capable of handling). Karma and obscurations are what prevent us from tuning in to the higher frequencies according to Buddhist teachings: the higher up we go the less limited we are by our physical-ness. Intelligence does not equate with the ability to tune in. In fact it can be a hindrance due to too much left brain activity getting in the way. Be aware then that a channel could be tuning in to an ego maniac whose information delivered only serves to confuse and seeks to satisfy its own desires. Be aware also that the channel will be manifesting a level of information relative to the channel's own understanding of who and what he or she is. A lower form of energy could not communicate via a high frequency channel.

Being Seen and Knowing It

The concept that we can be observed without observing is fascinating and explains much in the 'psychic' [12] world.

Whilst working at a house in Canberra I came the closest to seeing an observer than I had ever done before. I was called in to check out disturbing and limiting energy patterns in the house. The owner was not comfortable in the house and could not understand why. As we were talking in the dining area facing the passage through to the bedrooms, I saw a black shape dart out from the laundry and head off at high speed down the passage to an end bedroom. "What was that"? I asked. The owner replied, "Did you see it too. Thank goodness. "I thought I was going mad!" At last, the observer was observed. For many sensitive readers this may be a common, everyday occurrence but for those whose 'sight' is still within the 'normal' parameters it is encouraging. The dark shape was more an absence of light than a shadow and had been seen before by the householder.

I took off in pursuit and made brief contact. Occasionally these energy forms are elusive. It seems that when I start work with the pendulum and focus my awareness on energy patterns not in harmony with the greater environment, I radiate a bright energy. In my experience, shadows, ghosts, entities – whatever name we give to these energy patterns that are outside 'rational' explanation – are locked into the world between full physical manifestation and the astral or bardo realms by their own unexpressed or unacknowledged fears or desires. Fear energy, as we have mentioned before, is a low vibration which disturbs other energies within the environment. A fearful energy will endeavour to hide from a light source because of the fear which it may have experienced whilst still alive or around the time of death.

The energy pattern in the house in Canberra was definitely fear based. As you dowse on the different energy fields whilst scanning for disturbing frequencies, fear is easily recognised. That particular energy was quite mobile, limited to movement within the house but mobile none-the-less. Some, (but not all) of these patterns are mobile. Many seem to be locked into one particular spot in the environment, either inside a house, out in the paddock or in the bush or even possibly attached to a piece of furniture or artifact.

Changing the Energy Levels

It is the intensity of the emotion that dictates how dense an energy field such energies maintain. The stronger the emotion, the more attachment to some aspect of this third dimensional reality and consequently the more 'ghostlike' is the manifestation of the energy. The lower the vibration the more likely we are to see these energies. Moving up the scale to higher frequencies, we are no longer able to see but we can still 'feel' the energy patterns. Higher still and the energy patterns become subtle indeed. In the Canberra house (described above) I 'introduced' myself to this energy pattern, accepting that all is energy swimming around in a cosmic soup where there is no beginning and no end to anything or anyone and it is possible to communicate with one and all energy patterns, whether they have physical form or not. In the case of the energy in the Canberra house, the fear element which maintained a connection to the physical world was vibrating at too low a frequency to accept an input of higher energy and continued to avoid a connection with the energy that I represented.

I was discussing this disturbance with my client in the dining area when, with a rush of cold air, the shadow moved quickly past me. I only felt it this time but my client saw a complete manifestation move past her and became distressed. Fortunately friends were visiting and were able to comfort her. The energy pattern went into a corner in the family room and I was able to 'connect' with it easily. Focussing more light and thoughts of healing and love would be how I would have explained the process of 'clearing' a few years ago. Now I actually do very little, maintaining a state of being rather than an act of doing. Since I am able to hold the disturbing frequency without fear or judgement (this is most important), thereby raising the frequency of the disturbed energy pattern.

The effect is like heating water. When energy in the form of heat is applied to water it changes state. The applied energy excites the molecules to the degree they are able to break free from the main body of water and rise as a gas. When the heat (energy) goes out of water, it cools down. The molecules slow down as the water cools and the space between these molecules grows smaller until the water turns into ice.

It is much the same with disturbed frequencies, wherever and however they exist. Put more energy into them and inevitably they change state. Whilst they are in fear they may try and avoid receiving higher frequency energy, but sooner or later the balance tips and they start to 'lighten' up. The lighter they become the less the fear vibration is present, thus creating more light. The pattern soon changes to a much higher state and is no longer disturbing or affecting life in a 3D state.

On another occasion in Melbourne I was tracking energy flow through a house and the dowsing suddenly drew me upstairs. It was a dark evening and the couple who owned the house remained downstairs. As I moved along the upstairs passage way I felt I was moving into a cold energy field. My skin started to tingle and break out in goose bumps. This was a sure sign that I was approaching some focus point for a disturbance. Without warning the dowsing rod spun to my left and drew me quickly into the bathroom. Suddenly I felt as though I had walked into a refrigerator, so cold and fearful was the energy hiding away in the dark. I connected only momentarily with that energy pattern before returning to the ground floor and sharing my findings.

The owners stated that they had felt shivery each time they passed the bathroom, particularly at night, thereby confirming the presence of a disturbing pattern. A few moments later I felt a rush of energy move partially through my left side, leaving me very shivery: the entity had come downstairs, I dowsed it to be standing slightly behind me and to my left, in the corner of the room. It appeared to have become fed up with waiting for me. My earlier connection to it had put enough higher frequency energy into the slower frequencies that comprised this entity to move it out of fear and into a higher state. As the intensity of the energy increased so did the desire of the entity to acquire more of this higher frequency energy. Consequently it came to seek me out, not wanting to miss out on the opportunity of being released from the prison its fear had built for itself. The scales slowly tipped away from fear and less energy was required to maintain the process. A balance, or a higher vibration, was soon reached because the energy field had changed sufficiently to be able to continue the process of absorbing a higher frequency.

This is not a one-off encounter. There are many stories like this. The best way to realise the truth of my explanation is to put them to the test for yourselves. Do not accept anything I say at face value. Play with it for a while. If it feels good and sits right, test it to see if it works or not. It took me quite some time to come to these conclusions so do not be surprised if you take a long time to discover the truth of this for yourself or perhaps, in a flash of enlightenment, you come to understand this principle straight away.

These are many cases of almost tangible energy patterns to be found in homes and commercial buildings around the country. Other less obvious patterns are just as important affecting us and our environment. They are part of a blanket that covers us, shielding us from a greater light and thus are a factor in keeping us in a state of a fear vibration. As we come out of ignorance about these energy patterns and understand them for what they are, we realise that it is our own fear that is killing us, not the fear of the entity. We have the power to change our fears into a higher frequency. Energy patterns locked into the environment without a fully functioning physical, mental, emotional and spiritual body do not unlock themselves, at least not without someone who is without fear and judgement to help them on their way.

The Power of Thought, Word and Deed.

By living in fear then, by the law of attraction, we draw to ourselves that which we fear. Consequently the more we fear, the stronger the manifestation of the fear that we have to deal with. If we love, unconditionally, then we draw unconditional love to us. This is much more pleasant. Were we all living in unconditional love there would be no need for this book or the hundreds of others that are signposts back to love.

A few years ago I had a phone call from a young mother in the country. For some time she had a compulsion each time she went out on the back verandah to throw her young baby over it. This feeling grew and she became ever more fearful of it. On one level her fear was feeding this energy pattern. It was almost out of control when she rang me. The afternoon of the first phone call she experienced a disturbing energy come into the house behind her, filling the room with fear. Panicking, she screamed and broke down.

It was a particularly trying time for the young mother. The deeper into the fear she had gone, the harder it was to release its hold. With my assistance she was successful in moving beyond the fear and now lives happily. Had she sought help whilst that fear was in its embryonic stage it would have been much easier and much less painful to release it. If we focus on darkness, we soon forget what light is. By continuing to empower darkness in whatever form our imaginations direct, then we are empowering an emotion and propelling it to manifestation. If we keep going, then sooner or later we will have to deal with our emotion in a big way. Recognise that as we become conscious of the power of thought, word and deed, we are empowering ourselves to create consciously. We then make a choice: either to continue putting energy into fear, or to turn our thoughts to love (preferably unconditional, but we have to start somewhere).

Overcoming Fear

A big issue today for a lot of people is that they lack something, either a lack of freedom or a lack of money, lack of security, or whatever – it is all the same thing after you take away the labels. There are hundreds of 'abundance' books telling us how to manifest more of this and that into our lives. If they had the secret and it was that easy, would we need so many books? I know avid readers who have read almost everything about 'manifesting abundance', and are still reading. For me, abundance is what I have right now: my needs are met; the bills get paid; I have loving friends and a lifestyle designed around teaching, writing, bringing harmony back into homes and places of work, that is, built around all the things I love doing. There is no end to what would 'be nice' to have, but when is anyone ever satisfied? The sooner we start telling ourselves we are abundant now, the more abundant we will become.

The fear vibration is fundamental to most human experiences, even love. Many people love because they are afraid of being alone. Whilst we are afraid, there is little or no chance of us reaching the unity of consciousness.

"Our deepest fear", said Nelson Mandela, "is not that we are inadequate. Our deepest fear is that we are powerful beyond measure. It is our light, not our darkness, that most frightens us. We ask ourselves: who am I to be brilliant, gorgeous, talented, fabulous? Actually, who are you not to be?...Your playing small does not serve the world. There is nothing enlightened about shrinking so that other people won't feel insecure around you. We were born to manifest the glory that is within us. It is not just in some of us; it is in everyone. And as we let our own light shine, we unconsciously give other people permission to do the same. As we are liberated from our own fear, our presence automatically liberates others."

My deepest wish for many many years has been to manifest the glory that is within me by liberating myself from my fears so that others may be assisted in liberating their own fears. Nothing else matters but this, neither riches nor power. Everything comes and goes. Everything is left behind when the spark of life departs the body. We need to understand that everything, atoms, trees, planets, thoughts – is energy. This energy manifests as different frequencies which we can control in order to realise the absolute brilliance of our own light within.

Unless we lift the blanket that covers our heads we will miss the opportunity in every moment to rise above the limits imposed by fear. As Nelson Mandela states, "As we are liberated from our own fear, our presence automatically liberates others". We are not alone in battling our darkness. To think so is another part of the illusion of separation. There is no darkness and we are not doing battle. Confusion and addiction to illusion, however, still exist.

Explaining life in terms of energy, manifest (appearing in our third dimensional world) or unmanifest (formless, yet to appear), gives us a unique perspective and a greater ability to move beyond our limitations and so grow into the divine beings that we really are. Or to express it another way, we are already these divine beings and so we do not really have to grow into them. Instead we have to shed the skins of fear and confusion and realise our true nature. Energy frequencies are something tangible that we can deal with, something to understand and look at, something not to be afraid of.

The 'meaning of life', whenever and wherever it has been taught, has been either too cryptic or too simple. We try to decipher the cryptic and complicate the simple. What strange yet interesting beings we are. I hope that by seeing life in terms of energy we are able to avoid the cryptic, thus making the explanation so simple it leaves no room for complications. "It cannot be as easy as this!" some people might exclaim. Well, It is. It is very simple. A child trying to open a locked door would never succeed if it did not have the key. With the key – and a helping hand – the problem no longer exists.

The key is this: we are integrated parts of a whole entity. We affect the whole by our every thought, word and deed. Likewise the whole affects us, whether by the thoughts, words and deeds of other human beings, or by the animal, vegetable or mineral kingdoms, or by the higher frequency metaphysical energy patterns.

Nine

Releasing Death's Energies

Dying

How we die determines what happens to our consciousness
after physical death. The Tibetans have been aware of this
relationship for centuries; they have special ceremonies that
are designed to help guide the dead and release them from the
bonds of attachment to the living, that is, third dimensional
realm. If we die in fear, pain, anger, desire, or even with a
strong vision of heaven or hell then our thoughts and desires
will create our future beyond death due to the creative power
of thought and the attraction of similar frequencies. This cause
and effect scenario is not spiritual 'mumbo jumbo' but a
simple energy equation. We gather experiences like a
snowball rolling down a hill. Some experiences affect us more
than others and become integrated into who and what we
think we are.

Freeing the Despair of Suicides

Dowsing on a suicide energy pattern is an enlightening experience. To do this we have to be most sensitive and open to listening to our intuition. Too much logical or intellectual thought will effectively shield out the reception. There are three cases that come to mind, all different and all good examples of what can happen to the consciousness, or soul, after physical death.

The first was at an old coach station on the Adelaide – Strathalbyn run, long since given over to sheep and horses. The house was fronted by a courtyard with stables and outhouses opposite. A young religious woman who was the owner of the property was uncomfortable both in the house and in the courtyard after feeding the horses and shutting up the dogs, particularly at dusk, feeling as if she was being followed around the courtyard. This had gone on for many years and at times this feeling swelled and she would often yell out over her shoulder "Go away, leave me alone". She did not tell me this before I began working, perhaps a little embarrassed at her behaviour. When I dowsed the area I was caught up in a complex pattern threading around the courtyard. At no point did the energy flow go into the house. The energy flow just meandered, seemingly at random, around the courtyard. (When I dowse I generally ask for the direction of flow of the energy; in this case I was following the energy pattern, not retracing it to source.)

I knew that I had to get to the source of this energy pattern if I was to find out what was happening. Rephrasing my question, I asked to be shown where this energy was coming from, or what was its focal point, as it were. Retracing the path (still meandering) I was led to a small outbuilding at the end of the stables. On opening the door I saw a mental picture of a young lad, 18 or 19 years old, hanging from a rafter. For some reason, this young man had taken his life 145 years earlier, as I discovered through pendulum dowsing. For all those years he had been restricted to wandering in the courtyard, desperately lonely, asking (in this case my client) for help. She did not understand what was happening and felt fearful. She felt only his presence and was unaware of the trauma he was experiencing. If we recall that energy spinning at certain speeds can 'see' other energies of similar or lower speeds we can better understand how the energy of this young man was able to see my client (and me of course) and why we could not see him. His energy restricted no longer to physical form and hence a lower 'solid' energy pattern was able to vibrate at a higher speed, beyond our ability to see.

As I 'tuned' into this energy I felt the sadness and desperation of his years of being able to see but not be seen, to hear but not be heard, which must be most distressing for anyone caught up in such a place. Suicide is most definitely not an answer to life's problems. As we now understand, life continues after death. In fact, to take one's own life compounds the issues struggled with. If the person suiciding believes that death is the end and an escape from the terrors of life, imagine the dreadful realisation that death is not the end. The problems still remain because consciousness continues to unfold the drama it was caught up in prior to death. After death, it is much worse for the suicide because there is no-one to hear nor to listen and help, in fact no-one at all to share the burden.

Using a similar technique to that employed dealing with energy patterns locked into a specific place in the environment,

The Moment That Matters

I focussed healing energy into the consciousness of the young man. After a few moments a friend standing nearby felt cold chill surround her, immediately followed by a jolt of energy going through her body. This soon cleared and her energy returned to normal. According to my dowsing the energy had been released. I went inside to wash up and was overwhelmed by a powerful emotion of gratitude. Tears came to my eyes as the young man expressed his heartfelt thanks for the assistance I had been able to offer. Then, his energy lightening all the time, he was able to move on to continue his journey wherever that may be. My friend who had experienced the chill and the energy jolt felt that the young man's energy had passed through her, using her energy as a springboard to help it move beyond the limits previously constraining it.

A similar 'release' happened a few years later when I was called in to dowse and clear a suicide energy in a motel room in Queensland. At first I was surprised to find no trace of the man's energy left in the room since it is quite normal for the energy of a suicide to remain in the immediate vicinity of the death. I was asked to trauma counsel the staff members who found the body and discovered that the first person (a woman) who opened the door, which was still on the chain after the event, had felt a chill pass through her, followed by a jolt of energy. When I explained what had happened she was naturally concerned that the energy of the dead man might be lingering in her energy field, which can often happen. We were able to discover by dowsing that the energy had cleared almost immediately after she felt the chill and that there was no trace of the dead man's energy in her energy field, thus explaining why there was no evidence of the suicide present in the room.

In a more recent case using distant dowsing, I was asked to check the state of a young woman who had thrown herself from The Gap, a high cliff at the entrance to Sydney Harbour. The woman had gone missing on the Thursday night and the body was found on the Saturday. I was asked to help on the Monday morning. Tuning in to her consciousness I experienced an overwhelming feeling of greyness, cold and fear. It felt as though the young woman was wandering through a cold fog, lost and confused, seeking help but finding none. The fact that she was under medication would have added to her confusion. When I was able to 'connect' with her, the energy around the pendulum was extremely agitated and not its usual smooth motion at all. While I remained tuned into her energy the agitated pendulum indicated the high degree of confusion and distress she was experiencing. Calling on the understanding of non-local mind and the interconnectivity of all life we can question other energy patterns and can, through the pendulum or other means more naturally sensitive people may employ, communicate with those energies. Thus I was able to gain the attention of the wandering energy that had been the young woman and, through my energy, get her to listen to some soothing music we were playing at the time. When she focused on the music it was then necessary to give her something to look for, to lead her out of this fog in which she was trapped. I suggested she look for a bright light (the power of suggestion in this state so soon after death is quite strong). According to the Tibetan Buddhist tradition, the consciousness is far more responsive immediately after death, since it does not have the physical form and its limitations to hold it back. Also the consciousness that was the person is most receptive to thoughts and emotions, particularly of relatives and close friends.

In this case there were no relatives or close friends tuning in; perhaps no-one believed in any life after death. The woman was certainly receptive to my suggestions as I led her through the fog toward the light and I suggested at the same time that she look for a figure she recognised and was comfortable with. She agreed to do this and I was able to ease away from the connection. Still aware of her distress I asked that assistance continue even though I was not focussing consciously on the energy of the young woman. The following day when we checked the site again I found the pendulum to move in a very smooth motion,which was a good indication that the energy I was communicating with had stabilised. When asking if any more assistance was required I received a clear no: 'job complete'. As far as we have been able to ascertain, this woman's energy had cleared any connection to the physical world and had moved beyond the limiting confusing patterns of that particular after-death state. Had I, or someone with a similar awareness, not been asked to assist it is quite possible that the energy, that is, the consciousness of this young woman would still be wandering to this day in a purgatory of her own fears and confusions.

There is increasing concern over the number of young people suiciding and many organisations have been set up to help combat this rising pattern. I believe that if the awareness of the consciousness living on after physical death were made more public, then the suicide rate would drop drastically. Whilst people still think that death is the only answer to their problems, and while those problems are on the increase, then suicide might appear to be an option to living a life of pain. As greater understanding of the mystery of consciousness reaches more and more people, then alternatives to suicide must be considered. I think that even many of those now responsible for setting up organisations to deal with this problem are unaware of the reality of the situation. Energy consciousness continuing after death is perhaps considered too abstract a concept, with no 'scientific proof' to back it up, but this very important issue will continue to be ignored at too great an expense.

Unlocking A Violent Death's Energies

Suicide is quite a powerful energy and a person's energy or consciousness may be caught in a no-man's land for many years. But it is not the only type of energy that becomes locked in an in-between state. Sudden violent death can be just as distressing. There is an important difference between a suicide and cases of sudden violent death. Sudden violent death may be seen as a part of the karmic pattern, and hence destiny, of the person. Suicide (on one level) can also be seen as a part of the destiny of the person. If a person is tempted to suicide the cause is likely to be an issue that they are having considerable trouble dealing with. That issue must be faced sooner or later and moved beyond, or it will continue to grow and plague that person.

An interesting story that helps explain this point was recounted to me by a friend who is a past life regression therapist. A woman who had seemingly reached the end of her capacity to cope with a particular experience sought his help. Under hypnosis it was discovered that she had arrived at the same point ten times in previous experiences. Each time she had committed suicide thereby failing to learn the lesson, accept the situation and move beyond the old pattern. When she was informed of these past experiences after the session, she was better equipped to handle the problem and move beyond it, thus breaking a pattern that had lasted many lifetimes.

Sudden violent death can indicate a karmic pattern being realised, a lesson learnt and not to be repeated. Suicide is merely an evasion of an issue. Suicide creates greater dynamic tension between the person and the issue therefore guaranteeing a repeat performance in another lifetime. The more tension we create between ourselves and the issues that we continually refuse to face or are unable to deal with or simply do not recognise, then the bigger the hurdle becomes. It is always easier to deal with issues on whatever level whilst those issues are in an embryonic stage.

This concept can be described in the following way: as we move and grow we learn through life's experiences via our physical vehicle. The human body, developed over tens of thousands of years is the 'tool' without which we could not can gain these experiences. This tool has certain abilities and inbuilt memories: biological, racial and social to name but three; however we are not these memories. Memories are only the building blocks upon which we construct and add to our experiences. The foundations of biological, racial and social memories are important to what and how we experience that which life presents us with but they are not us. We tend to identify with those memories and may say that they are us (or we them), but who we really are goes way beyond these memory patterns. We might even say that we are our experienced memories, but if we followed this line to its ultimate conclusion then all we are is a complex bunch of memories, including memories of other experiences (lives) that are prominent in the current make-up, or a collection of memories that we think ourselves to be now. Rather we are the creator and experiencer, the one who is experiencing life's games. It is the consciousness that inhabits the body, because the body is a physical being caught up in time and space and is the tool through which we experience life – a life subject to the experiences of the body/consciousness. Experiences may be pleasant or otherwise, depending upon the memories we have of similar experiences. Here our emotional body has a big say in how we react to different experiences. If I were born in the countries of the Middle East my associated experiences around bartering would be quite different had I been born in a European culture. A different racial, social or religious view on the same fundamental issue would prompt a different emotional response. Neither happens to be right or wrong, just different.

A Pebble Grows

Certain standards impose themselves and govern my reactions to different emotional stimuli. If in my journey through a life I encounter something which, because of a particular way I have of looking at life I would rather not deal with, I sidestep the issue. At this stage the issue is just a pebble in the road: because we set ourselves certain lessons due to our attachment to certain beliefs, that pebble will present itself on our path yet again. The next time the issue arises it has developed into a small rock. Because we have not dealt with the issue we have created more dynamic tension between the lesson or issue in the sense that due to our denial or refusal to face that issue we have empowered it a little more. Still avoiding that issue, the next time we encounter it the issue appears as a larger rock, then a still larger rock that is not so easy to sidestep. The next time it may become a wall which we will certainly have difficulty in negotiating. All the time it becomes more and more difficult to deal with the original issue which started out as just a little pebble.

Many different means will show up to make us look at the original issue and move beyond its lessons. Physical sickness is one of those lessons, being the end result of refusing to deal with a 'pebble'. Had we but dealt with the issue cleanly and clearly in its early stages then we would have negated the need to deal with the mountain. Recall the woman and her manifesting fear that was compelling her to throw her baby over the verandah.

The Video Plays On

Sudden violent death may well be the manifestation of a minor issue blown out of all proportion by our refusal to see or deal with a particular issue, a way of repaying a karmic debt, as it were. It is also important to note that a person suffering a sudden violent death still has the video playing. We tend to live either in the past or the future due largely to our inability to live completely in the moment, possessing a dire lack of awareness regarding experience of the consciousness after death.

For most of us our future is built moment by moment on our past experiences. Simple memories of work and leisure activities, responsibilities and family life impose a sort of autonomous script which we follow blindly because of their regularity. Our perceived needs for security ensure a regular pattern to our lives. If we die unexpectedly, this pattern, so well entrenched in the consciousness, will continue to play. The shocked mind continues to play out familiar patterns. Fear and confusion set in when no-one can see or hear the departed. Inability to accept physical death, more so for those who have no concept of an 'after-life', prevents the consciousness releasing its hold on third dimensional reality.

In its strongest sense this hold on 3D reality is the starting point for the manifestation of a ghost haunting a place. Attachment to a particular place, for whatever reason, even a piece of furniture, is sufficient bonding for an energy (in the form of a ghost) to remain locked into that environment. On a lesser scale the threads of energy that connect us all (the Web of Indra) seem to remain. This is evident in the cases of suicide or sudden violent death, connecting the place of death to that person's home or loved ones. These energy lines can be dowsed upon, using the dowsing process to open up and become receptive to out total environment, little by little communicating or accessing the information contained in the energy line. Through this process we can understand more about these energy lines and therefore more about ourselves. Two examples come to mind. Whilst staying overnight with friends I slept in a room in which I had never slept before. As I lay down to sleep, relaxing my body and mind, I suddenly had a very clear mind picture of being in an accident and dying. I did not attach a great deal of importance to this, but moments later another picture entered my mind. I imagined myself hovering 30 metres or so above the ground looking down. I saw a white utility and 'knew' I was travelling in this car. Ahead and out of site of the driver in the car, a truck went out of control. The utility came around the corner and crashed into the truck. The occupant of the utility ('me') died in the accident. I thought little more about it, however although the whole episode seemed strange and out of character. I released the thought from my conscious mind and went to sleep.

The following day I checked, using a dowsing rod, for any metaphysical energy lines passing through the room. I found, not surprisingly, one line passing through the corner of the bed where my head had lain the night before. Tuning in to this energy pattern using the pendulum for my yes/no answers and following my intuition as questions presented themselves, I was able to discover more details. The line had been created by a young man who, having died a sudden violent death in the car crash, sought out the familiarity of his home environment. His video of his life was still playing. Habit had taken over from 'reality' and he was seeking to find safety and reason in his everyday activities. The line that I had tuned into the night before was connecting the place of the accident with his home and contained information in the form of consciousness or a pattern of vibrational energy. I had interpreted that information correctly.

The next example gives us an idea of the intensity of these energy patterns and how they can and do effect people living in the path of such energies. I was called in to check out a disturbance in a friend's house which was near a site of significant Koori (Aboriginal) interest. The house had been comfortable for many years but had recently taken on an underlying vibration that was affecting the woman of the house especially. Checking with the dowsing rod (and keeping in mind that dowsing requires us to open up our defences, that is, become as receptive as we are able in order to access the information we are seeking) I discovered two narrow energy lines passing through the house. Both lines were coming from the Koori site. I made a connection with each line. One passed through the dining table where I was seated, marking the line on a floor plan of the house for the owners. As I was sitting there I noticed a distinct ringing in my ears, followed by an echoing inside my head. These internal noises grew stronger to the point where although I could clearly hear the words of a person talking in my left ear whilst he was standing at a distance from my right side, I could not hear him immediately on my left at all. I tried different methods to clear myself, but without success. This occurred at 2.30 p.m We left the house at 3.30 and it was not until 10.30 that night that the symptoms subsided and I lost the ringing noise and regained my hearing.

The Diverse Ways of Knowing

If both cases (described above) were to happen every night, or each time you passed through your dining room and you had no idea where they were coming from or why, you would soon be seeking medical advice. But what could any doctor or therapist find? Since nothing tangible existed, you may well be told that "it is all in the mind". Well, everything is in the mind; it cannot be anywhere else for us to access it, but this does not help understand why it was in my mind and no-one else's. I tuned in specifically to these energies. Most of us would only touch upon them briefly and the symptoms would not be as severe as if we intentionally went right into them to understand more. Without foreknowledge of the existence of this energy it becomes difficult to move beyond the symptoms. An awareness of the world we live within goes a long way to remove the fear that arises because of the unknown. Fear is like an impenetrable fog drifting at the limits of our awareness.

There are many other examples of this type of energy pattern, each slightly different depending upon the emotion or thought and the intensity with which the emotion or thought was produced. These lines criss-cross the environment, passing through houses and offices with no difficulty at all. If we spend time within one or more of these energy lines we are affected, to whatever degree, by the information contained within that line. Most times the effect is so subtle that we are not even aware of it, still it continues to affect us, often significantly. Whether the effect is on the physical level, the emotional or mental depends greatly on the frequencies of the energy field and our personal response to that range of frequencies. Also what may adversely affect one person may not disturb another at all, a factor to take into account when trying to understand the nature of the disturbance. Whereas we are all in bodies that are basically the same, some are affected by things that others do not even notice due to the way we imagine ourselves, our limitations, our perceptions of reality, our karma and obscurations. In this sense each of us is so unique that no blanket statement or diagnosis can categorise various states of disease, whether physical, emotional or mental.

The Domino Effect

If we look for conclusive proof that a particular energy pattern has a particular effect on us we will be most disappointed. For example it is difficult at this point in time to blame Extremely Low Frequency Electro-Magnetic Radiation as a sole cause for leukemia. Some people are affected while others are not and some more so than others, each in slightly different ways. So it is with all other disturbing energy patterns. Food poisoning may affect one group but not another. Why is this so? Certainly when a case of food poisoning receives a great deal of publicity our collective fears take over, while those people who have eaten potentially contaminated food, whether they were showing signs of sickness or not, will soon manifest those symptoms and end up quite sick.

Experiments in various work-places have demonstrated the effect of contagion via the power of thought. A person in the workplace might complain of dizziness, nausea and then, after building upon these symptoms for a day or two, suddenly and dramatically collapse in front of work-mates and be rushed away, presumably to receive medical attention. Within a day or two, another person in the workplace might repeat the performance. This occurrence might then be enough for others in the workplace to experience the same symptoms, some with varying degrees of authenticity depending on how accurately the explanation of the symptoms had been relayed from person to person throughout the work-force.

The first two cases (as related above) were once 'created' to observe the effects such a dramatic illness might have on work colleagues. Within weeks, dozens of employees were suffering the same symptoms. Wayne Dyer relates the story of a doctor who was curing AIDS patients regularly before the issue went public and headlines of 'killer virus' spread around the world. After this media attention, more and more deaths followed. We are incredibly sensitive creatures, and whilst we harbour fears within our being then we will easily succumb to the fears generated by an irresponsible few.

There are of course many layers to this perspective. Naturally a virus has a life of its own. Whether or not that virus gets beyond our defence system is another matter. We can look at the mechanics of the body for an answer but we need to look further for a reason why the body behaves a particular way. In the book "A Course in Miracles" [13] they frequently refer to "All healing is essentially release from fear". What I am proposing here are different perspectives to reality, that is, perspectives based on understanding, not fear or lack of knowledge. My perspectives are different to those normally offered in that they are based on pure energy. The explanations given here are designed to raise people above any remaining fears they may have.

The point I would like to emphasise is that fear is all that stands between us and freedom and that fear does not die with physical death. In the examples given concerning suicide and sudden violent death we are able to build up a picture of consciousness within and outside of the physical body. Consciousness is not the physical body – the body is a tool through which consciousness experiences. If a pattern of fear develops due to the consciousness inhabiting a physical body which itself has needs, desires, hopes and expectations, then that fear is like a veil hung across the face of consciousness. Consciousness must then see life through the veil. Pure consciousness knows no veil, since it is our imagination driven by fears and loss that will construct the veil. When the physical form dies the veil lives on, depending upon the intensity with which it was created and maintained. It also depends upon the spiritual awareness of the individual and their ability or otherwise to live totally in the moment and not create their future based on the fears of the past. This is not so easy to do, and I will explore this aspect further in the section on dowsing on the physical, emotional and mental (see the chapter on Dowsing One To One page 141).

Energy Imprints

An energy imprint can be imposed upon the physical environment at any time and place. Often the cause for such imprints are strong emotional energy releases based on a mis-understanding of the nature of reality. Energetic imprints are laid down during life, especially when we are unable to recognise or forgive a person, place or event, and they are sustained by our own lack of awareness via the energy threads or lines we looked at earlier. For example we might move house but leave our energy patterns behind for another to experience. If we are unable to forgive a person or release that person from a possessive love then the energy thread will continue to connect us to them even after one or both persons die.

These energy patterns can be disturbing for other people who unknowingly move into the house, office or environment that still holds such patterns. When the energy we take with us (such as the excitement of moving house etc) settles down, we begin to experience the energy of the new environment. In the first days or months we seem to be immune from the energy patterns in the new environment because our reserves maintain our old energy patterns. But as we spend a longer time in the new environment we become more sensitive to the energy patterns it holds.

Energy patterns relate to different levels or frequencies of energy. From the ground up we have the earth's energies such as the magnetic fields within the earth, underground water, geological fault lines and underground caves which can affect our health and well-being without our being aware of their existence. Moving higher up the frequency range, we pass through the field of technological disturbances which may, or may not be more pronounced in a new environment. Factors affecting change in the technological energy patterns in an environment depend upon proximity to power lines, transformers, micro-wave repeater stations, effective earthing of the domestic power supply and any change in the use of electrical appliances. What can change when people move into a new environment is the total number of stress factors in their lives and the consequent assault on the immune system which is then unable to cope with all these energy fields.

More important than the earth's energies and technological fields, however, are the energy imprints containing emotional and mental memory patterns. The longer we spend in areas of such distress, the more likely we are to be affected by these energy imprints. Emotional stress held in the environment impacts severely on occupants living in such an energy field. The degree to which individuals will be affected depends on the personal issues the individual is dealing with at the time and their response to particular frequency patterns. An emotionally sensitive person is more likely to be adversely affected by a disturbing environmental energy pattern than a person whose heart centre is not open at all. A person with the closed heart will also be affected, although the symptoms will not be as obvious and certainly, when symptoms do occur, they will not be consciously linked with any environmental disturbance.

Energy Pattern Disturbances

Where a disturbance is severe as was the case of the energy patterns in a unit in Brisbane that I was called in to clear, anyone living in such a place would feel the effects over a short time, but not know the cause. In that particular unit the dowsing led me to all the cupboards and wardrobes in the house, ending within each wardrobe in a tight spiral formation. Tuning in to each of the spiral patterns, I felt an increasing level of fear and abuse. The picture I saw, or rather felt, was one of a young child hiding or being kept shut in the wardrobes. In the centre of the living room was an intense pattern of terror and abuse. I picked up this disturbance strongly; it was also accompanied by a cold shivering and strong feeling of revulsion. It seemed as if a young girl had been physically and mentally abused in this house. The energy patterns of the fear, being so strong, had remained in the environment and were affecting the emotional health of the man living in the unit at the time.

Another severe case where an energy was seriously affecting the emotional and mental health of people in the environment was in a nightclub. The nightclub was below ground level and had no natural lighting. It was quite dark when I went down into the nightclub. Psychics and other sensitive people had been unable to spend more than three minutes in the nightclub without having to escape the disturbing feelings contained there. Of particular interest was the fact that these same people could not get within ten metres of the women's toilets without feeling extremely agitated and distressed.

When picking up the lines of distress, the dowsing led me directly to the women's toilets. The closer I got the more uncomfortable I felt. My skin began breaking out in goosebumps. My stomach tightened. The closer I got to the toilet the more intense was the disturbance. The feeling I had was of fear and stress. I finally reached the focal point of the energy pattern in one of the toilet cubicles. The feeling here was quite overpowering. A sense of desperation, fear and loneliness washed strongly through my energy field. After opening myself up to it I wondered why I picked such a vocation as dowsing!

I spent considerable time focussing energy into the disturbed frequency of the pattern in the toilet. Gradually the disturbed feelings started to lessen until they reached a point where they were having no adverse effect upon their environment. Soon the disturbed pattern had cleared completely. I was told later that a young woman had died of an asthma attack in that cubicle. One can only imagine the fear and pain she must have gone through. But now it was good news for the psychics and sensitives who were able to spend time in the nightclub and even use the toilet. And more good news for the owner who later sold the business, since until then all attempts at selling had failed.

These examples demonstrate that energy of a metaphysical nature can affect life in the third dimension on many levels. This is due to the fact that there is no separation between these 'realities'.

Understanding A Country's History

We in Australia are lucky in that the layer, or blanket of disturbance, is a lot thinner here than in some countries. White settlement covers only two hundred years and it is in this short period that a lot of the man-made disturbance has occurred. Prior to white settlement, the energy of the native Kooris was very much in harmony with their environment. Energy patterns were also laid down by the Kooris and there are many sacred and significant sites, routes across the land, camp sites and burial sites that have their very strong energy patterns. This is to be expected from a culture that has had a strong belief for tens of thousands of years in the Dreamtime, that is, the origin, cause and maintenance of creation.

I stated previously that energy patterns or imprints are laid down by the living. In our culture the dead have little ability to lay down such patterns and no energy to sustain them. In Koori culture, their belief is strong in the two realities existing side by side. For a Koori to be in more than one place or reality at a time is something the western mind finds difficult to grasp, yet it is second nature to those who have maintained their belief over many centuries and, for the energy dowser, that world is only just beginning to open up. The Koori world contains the well guarded secrets of the Dreamtime as well as the concepts of a belief that has lasted tens of thousands of years.

The Moment That Matters

Over the past 200 years migrant Australians have come into a land of promise: "the lucky country". For years many of these early migrants had little or no understanding of the indigenous peoples who have lived in relative harmony in this land for thousands of years. In a typically colonial manner the new arrivals took whatever they wanted, abusing the local original inhabitants and then converting them to Christianity by whatever means they felt desirable. Riding roughshod over the sensitivities of the local inhabitants is a typical trait of all colonising powers and in many cases the social order that follows is built on shaky foundations. To reach and maintain any state (which in the process degrades any other state) can be likened to the biblical reference of building a house on sand. Without a deep awareness and sensitivity to the energy of the land and its keepers, as the Koori indigenous cultures have maintained, there can be no lasting connection. Trying to superimpose a culture by indoctrinating the local populace into the colonising culture's religions and 'socially acceptable' behaviour patterns is a typically western band-aid approach.

The spirituality of the indigenous cultures may have been whitewashed over but the essence of it is so deeply imbedded in the very nature of the land that it will take more than a paintbrush to create a new sustainable culture. The energy that is the land in this most ancient of continents is ever present. It is always ready to cross the reality barrier, stirring up thoughts and emotions deep within those that dwell here.

Some Historical Causes of Disturbances

There are many cases where people have built their houses, offices and factories with no real understanding of the land. This applies to Australia as much to any western, eastern or oriental country where the developers have lost touch with their roots, that is, their connection to the earth and the consciousness it contains.

Many problems arise if we thoughtlessly develop our way across the land in order to make profit the major factor in any undertaking. Profit rules out sensitivity. Shareholders want results in the form of dividends. Sensitivity to the environment, regrettably, pays no such short term dividends. Lack of sensitivity guarantees a most unsustainable future – as we are currently witnessing. Abuse on any level, whether to other people, creatures, plant life or planet is highly unsustainable. If it is said that "we learn by our mistakes", how many mistakes do we need to make?

I have encountered several cases where a client, through a lack of awareness, has suffered the effects of their environment. These cases include continuous problems in the planning stages of a building, ill health, accidents caused by and to the builder of the house, and misfortune and ill health of the occupants of the building. The land designated for the building may well have been a Koori burial site, a sacred site or a place of initiation. In all cases it is as though we are trying to bulldoze through a thought pattern which we do not know even exists. In addition many developers could not care less. Only if we are aware of the energy pattern can we equip ourselves to deal with it.

In some cases it is possible to 'negotiate' a settlement. Sensitivity and awareness, respect and protocol are all that are required most times. Prolonged health problems, for example, may be a result of living over an area of Koori significance. A friend reported that whilst living in New Zealand a particular family had seemingly endless health, financial and relationship problems, also accidents whilst living over an area that they later discovered to be a Maori burial site. What happened was not a figment of a fanciful imagination but was related to an almost tangible energy field whose reality is imposing itself into the world of the human third dimension.

Some Historical Causes of Blocked Energy Flow

Links between the living and the dead may be difficult to accept if we have no true understanding that, on a consciousness level, there is little difference between the two states. I have investigated too many cases where the energy of an environment was affected and consequently changed as a result of some form of karmic connection.

Ill health and even a lack of a social life can be the result of blocked energy flow through a house or property. One client, for example, had been attracted to a specific area repeatedly whilst horse riding and eventually bought a property close to that area, but her mother was unable to stay in the new house. An uneasy feeling which her mother could not explain kept her away. Then health problems began to manifest for my client and there was a sharp drop in the usual level of social contact at the house.

When I checked out the energy flow I found that the Qi, or Life Force, did not enter the property from the gate off the roadside. This is not uncommon but happens only in a small number of cases. When I went back in time, (keep in mind that dowsing accesses a conscious state that is beyond time and space) I found that the Qi energy flowed freely onto the property through the fence. This was an interesting observation. I was told that the previous owners had their gate precisely where the energy flow entered the property. Having established that the energy had stopped moving onto the land when my client purchased the property it was quite obvious that she had, in some way, been responsible for this change.

There are many questions to ask in such a situation but the problem in this case seemed to lie at the place my client had frequently visited prior to moving into the area. I mentioned this to her and she replied that she had been told that local Koori people were driven off the cliff to their deaths. We drove to the cliff site after I had dowsed a strong connection between my client and the Koori people who had suffered there. I spent considerable time healing and clearing disturbing patterns in the area. Upon returning to the property I checked and confirmed that the energy flow had returned. An effect of this 'healing' was that my client's social life returned quickly to its normal high level and her health began to improve.

A similar case of connecting with the Koori energy of a site occurred whilst working on a property in the New England Ranges. Changing the energy in that particular environment was quite difficult. I had a strong impression that there was something I needed to do in return for the co-operation of the Koori people connected to that site. At the time it was not clear what the 'favour' was, but the energy of the site cleared, much to the occupants relief. Later, whilst discussing this situation, another particular site was mentioned where, again, local people had been thrown from a bluff to their deaths. I passed this site a few days later and spent some time clearing and healing and thus returned the favour.

Another instance, but on a more individual scale, occurred when the owners of a house in the Dandenong Ranges were having considerable trouble completing an extension to their house. After dowsing the area, it was clear to me that an area of Koori significance was involved. An awareness of this energy could have saved a lot of problems in the early stages of the development. Once the owners realised the problem, and I was able to 'negotiate' on their behalf, the situation changed quickly and the renovations went ahead. I then asked the owners to hold the local energy in mind during their regular meditations and to be aware of protocol in order to maintain a good relationship with the energies of the environment.

Healing Required

Where great antagonism has created a gulf between peoples then forgiveness is extremely difficult to achieve, however much it may be necessary.

Anger, fear, frustration rage and humiliation are powerful emotions. When there is unforgiveness, combined with one or other of the party's lack of awareness of what it is they are doing, then a strong emotional energy remains in the environment, imprinting itself in the vicinity of the cause. The more sensitive we become, the more we begin to feel our environment in a way that we may have denied ourselves before. At first the feelings are so subtle we do not distinguish them as separate from our own thoughts or emotions. The feelings become us and we become them. Intermingling thoughts and feelings begin to struggle for supremacy. If we are not awake to what is happening and start to identify with all of the thoughts and emotions we are experiencing then we take on those thoughts and emotions. However where there is considerable difference between our 'truer' nature and the imprinting energies of our environment, the result may be schizophrenic, thus causing an inner argument over what is real and what is not. Ultimately all is real. It is the power behind identifying with any aspect of our perceived reality that creates the conflict.

Certain areas that I have been asked to check out have been male Koori energy centres, in which women find it difficult to live harmoniously, even to the extent that they cannot enter certain rooms in the house. Once a mother I worked for could not go into her son's bedroom, even to tidy up. There was a strong presence of a male energy area in that room that was affecting the son as well as effectively keeping the mother from the room. In other cases there are strong female centres, resting places or birthing areas which will reject male energy. This creates many problems for men living in the area (and for women too who do not understand the energy of the area). I find such areas to be passive and high in the Yin qualities. They are not good locations for business and even the occupants of a home may suffer lack of motivation and drive even poor health and financial worries if they live too long in such an area.

The Moment That Matters

At one time I was called in by a family where the wife and child had felt and seen a Koori male energy in the house, which was more noticeable when the husband was away on business. This was an extremely distressing experience for the woman and child. No one in the family would venture into the back yard after dark for any reason. They felt that there were a group of Koori males waiting in the darkness and this feeling was so strong that there was a high level of fear associated with it. When I tried to access the information, whilst sitting at the dining table in the house, I received no clear response from the pendulum. Only by moving outside the house did I obtain a response, but, try as I might with the dowsing rod, I could not access an energy flow into the house. The flow not only stopped at the front door, it felt as if an invisible energy field was blocking the door and preventing me from entering. In a case like this I try to make contact with the disturbing energy and gradually transfer healing energy (light) into the disturbing pattern. As I began doing this, standing with the owner on the verandah facing the front door to the house, I felt a rush of cold air. At that moment the woman took a step back in fright – she could see the male energy inside the front door. She said he told us to go away and leave him in peace in this house and that he meant no harm. The woman was quite shaken, so I continued to dowse on the male Koori's energy pattern. Slowly but surely I moved into the house, metre by metre until we arrived in one of the children's bedrooms and made contact with the focal point of the energy pattern. After more work the pattern dissolved and cleared. Checking the garden again, I found no trace of the group of Kooris who seemed to have been connected with the male energy inside the house. Once he left there was no reason for them to remain.

These types of experience are happening to more and more people coming from all walks of life. Once it was only 'mediums' and 'psychics' who were in touch with these energies. Now there is no telling who will see or feel or hear such energies.

It is my view that the veil that separates our world from the world of the higher, unseen vibrations grows thinner day by day. The borders of the one overflow over into the other. This situation of course, has always been the case because there is no separation other than the barriers we have built to keep us 'safe' from the horrors of the unseen worlds. It is these barriers that are dissolving.

Poltergeist Activity

Another interesting phenomena that affects the energy balance in a house is poltergeist energy which is commonly observed as objects flying through the air with no obvious means of propulsion. This phenomenon can be explained in energy terms to de-mystify the poltergeist activity and helps remove any fear that may be produced in the mind of the observer.

Anywhere that energy is dammed up, great pressure is produced. The analogy of a 'dam' illustrates this point well. Water held back by a dam wall creates huge pressure. When water is released and passes through a turbine, electricity is generated. If the water supply was kept up but the water in the dam was not released, there would come a point when the pressure of the water would burst the dam. This is the principle on which I believe the poltergeist phenomenon is based. Generally energy of an emotional nature, dammed up and unexpressed inside a person, (alive or dead), reaches a point where it can not be contained any longer. This energy then expresses its pent up feelings by creating havoc in the environment, as the following example highlights.

I was called in to check the energy influences in a house and was able to restore balance back to the environment with little difficulty. The husband was a proud and self reliant man, formerly in the army, but was adversely affected by a stroke and given to bad moods and depression. Because he was unable to care for himself completely or enjoy his retirement fully, he became more and more introspective. My usual procedures when looking at the energy patterns in a house are to check out the owner/occupiers as well. In his case there was considerable anger and resentment stored in his emotional energy field. When this energy pattern was released, there appeared nothing further for me to do.

Shortly after my visit, however, I heard from his daughter that poltergeist phenomena had started to occur in the house. Books flew around the room as though thrown in anger. I soon discovered that the father's pent up emotional energy was being released via the poltergeist activities. Working further on his emotional energy body I was able to stabilise this disturbance and release all the built up tension that was the cause for the poltergeist activities. After that session there was no further evidence of poltergeist activity.

In another, but less dramatic situation, a young man who attended one of my weekend workshops had a similar experience. A keen and excited student, he had returned home most enthusiastic after the weekend. Working with the energy patterns in his home he cleared and restored balance wherever it was needed. However in the process of clearing he altered the energy balance in the environment (in the act of restoring a more harmonious balance). A few days later he rang me to say that whilst in the house with a friend, glasses in a cabinet behind him had started to rattle and move about but no other evidence of disturbance was evident. This movement developed to the point where one glass flew out of the cabinet and hit him on the head. His friend was most upset. I discovered that by the work he did to restore an harmonious balance to the environment he had simultaneously released a great deal of tension that was stored in that environment. We did not look into the original cause which may have been the emotional disturbance of a previous owner occupier, or Koori energy or trauma stored in the consciousness of the land itself. A little more dowsing and focussed energy soon cleared the pattern and there was no further recurrence of the phenomenon.

Interestingly poltergeist activity is often found in the vicinity of pubescent girls, and, to a much lesser degree pubescent boys. Emotional turmoil and the inability, for whatever reason, to express that turmoil can result in poltergeist actions. If the emotional stress is dealt with, whatever its origin including the energy of a deceased person, then the phenomenon will reduce and not return. As long as the cause is still 'injecting' charged emotional energy into the environment, the poltergeist activities will continue. If there is no understanding and only fear in those who witness such events, then there is little chance of a reduction of these activities.

10

Dowsing Buildings and Homes

Environmental Factors

There are many aspects of the environment that need to be taken into account when planning a building: Some are obvious; others are only now coming into the awareness of the western mind. As a result of the growing interest to build in harmony with the environment, Feng Shui, which is the Chinese eco-art of living in harmony with our environment, is gaining popularity in the west. Whereas anything that increases general awareness of harmonious living is worth considering, attachment to another culture's beliefs can present problems. Amongst the useful information contained under the general heading Feng Shui, there is a great deal of superstition. As the ever hungry mind of the West seeks to understand itself better, it breaks away from orthodox beliefs and explores Eastern or Oriental thought in the hope of finding answers in the cultures of other lands. Yet if we look more objectively at those other cultures we see why they have evolved as they have. We also see that they have their own problems and are really no closer to any real answer than we are. Why then should we turn our attention to the spiritual or philosophic practices of other cultures?

Many major spiritual and philosophical works tell us that "the answer lies within", but repeatedly we ignore this information and seek answers, if not outside our own back door, then the back door of another and more exotic culture. Clutching at another culture's straws may expand our knowledge but in the long run it does little to expand our wisdom. However we can still learn much in the Feng Shui traditions. This information can be put to good use and enhance our sense of well being, but it is not information that is going to solve all our problems. We must realise that our problems (if indeed we really have any) are contained within us, that they are us and are a result of who and what we think we are, including our karma and obscurations. We are the only people who can face our problems and change our reality. Where we put our bed or kitchen is only a cosmetics exercise if we fail to see where the problem really lies.

Searching For Stress Lines

In Germany there is an Institute for Building Biology and Ecology, which is an organisation devoted to environmentally safe building practices. At the top of their list is: "Call in the dowser!" Before buying, planning or building it is necessary to have a clear picture of the energy of the land. Some places will enhance the proposed use of the building; some will create unnecessary stress. You need to know if any geo-pathic stress is evident. If you build over a stressed physical environment you can expect that stress to manifest in your lives at some time or other. If you build too close to high tension power lines and find that you, or a member of your family, is overly sensitive to this type of energy field and that sickness follows, wouldn't you have been better knowing this before you bought or built? If the land that you are thinking of purchasing was a Koori burial site, would you still be happy to live there? Amongst the energy threads or lines that criss cross the planet, many in Australia are the result of Koori consciousness. These lines connect sacred places or might be a regular path at certain times of the year for a particular group of people or be major energy lines which support the integrity of the environment. If you have one or more of these lines passing through your house or property you can expect to feel the energy contained in the line at various times.

People with clairvoyant abilities can sometimes see forms walking along the energy lines. Others less gifted might have a sense or feeling of someone passing through the room. This feeling can be quite disconcerting, especially if the line passes through the bedroom. Foreknowledge is important. In many cases it is possible to live in harmony with these energy patterns but for the more sensitive or fearful it is better not to build over them in the first place.

It is interesting to note that when dealing with various metaphysical disturbances, the energy thread that connects them retracts along its course, like a fishing line being reeled in when the pattern is cleared and harmony is restored to the environment. Having picked up on a line of 'disturbed' energy it is possible to follow it to a point where it is anchored in third dimensional space/time. Standing on this anchorage point and allowing healing energy to flood into the disturbed pattern, the pattern will increase in frequency. When this energy reaches 'lift off' frequency, namely when the energy is vibrating at too high a frequency to remain locked in to dense energy fields, the decreasing spiral (indicative of the focal point of the disturbing pattern) starts to decompress.

This effect can be experienced by dowsing over the energy pattern's focal point and then looking for that point a couple of minutes later, and then a few minutes later again. Not only does the spiral decompress but it retraces its path and moves out of the house or environment it was locked in at the time it was released. As the energy pattern moves out of the environment, the Qi (life force) that passes through the house is freed up a little more, enhancing the nature of the house. This exit can be quite powerful, depending on the intensity of the disturbance causing the problem [14].

Occupants – Past and Present

A fascinating point to take into account here is the different nature of the various disturbing patterns. When energy-dowsing a house there are several categories of metaphysical disturbance that I check for, on the assumption that a disturbing pattern is present. Firstly I ask if the disturbing areas are (or were) caused by the current occupants of the house. Strong negativity, emotional imbalance, fear or anger or depression can all be traced back to someone at some time or other. If an occupant or an acquaintance of the current occupiers is responsible for any of the disturbing patterns, then the pattern itself will need clearing. Moreover, the person responsible will need to be informed and cleared wherever possible so that they do not continue to set up these disturbing patterns. When people realise what they are doing and the effect it is having upon our environment, they are more likely to try and change their ways. Motivation must come from an inner knowing and not from someone else that may or may not know better.

After having looked at any areas of disturbance created by current occupants, I then turn to previous occupants and their friends or relatives. I should explain that when any example of past disturbance is found and cleared it is highly unlikely that it will return. The energy that put it there and kept it in place is not available anymore and consequently the pattern will return to its source. However, if a person who was responsible for creating a disturbed pattern in a house is still alive and is still focussed on that place (for whatever reason), then it is possible (but only remotely) that the energy disturbance might return. For example a house in Melbourne that sold considerably below the market price due to the dire straits of the previous owners was the target of anger and frustration on the part of those owners. The energy was cleared but a week later the old patterns were back. Here the intensity of the emotion, coupled with the fact that the previous owners responsible for the disturbance were still alive and still angry, made sure the negative patterns were reintroduced.

During the time that a pattern laid down by a previous owner occupier is released it is possible to trace its path as it returns to its source. This energy always moves through the rooms, doorways and passages of the house to exit at the front or back door. When dealing with energy patterns that pre-date the current building, (from Koori groups or early settlers in Australia's case), the lines, as they return to source, may pass through the walls or windows since in the consciousness of the person or persons responsible for creating the lines, the building did not exist at the time the energy pattern was formed. An interesting example is quoted by Dr. Hiroshi Motoyama in his book Karma and Reincarnation [15]. As a monk with significant powers of meditation, Motoyama was able to access places in space and time of which most of us are not aware. One incident he relates explains this point. Motoyama's shrine and institution are located on a tract of land bordering a beautiful park in Tokyo. Motoyama detected a very old soul exerting a protective influence over the property. Entering a deep state of meditation called 'Samadhi', Motoyama was able to discover that the site of the shrine had been the home of a powerful tribal leader 3,500 years earlier. It appeared that the warlord had re-created, in a higher astral sense, his reality which he was playing over and over again. This energy pattern was superimposing itself on the environment, thus influencing the here and now. To the occupants of the institution they were in a beautiful area of a Japanese city; but the warlord was still back in the little touched, natural environment that was his reality 3,500 years ago.

This tale illustrates the importance of a person's consciousness laying down a particular pattern and the attachment he or she may have to that pattern. We all leave threads of energy behind us as we go about our daily business. These threads are dowsable depending upon the intensity of the emotion and the sensitivity of the dowser. Most of these threads are fine and subtle and will eventually fade into nothingness. It is the more energised threads that we pick up as disturbances in our environment that concern us here. It shows that we are affected by energies in our environment of which we had previously been unaware. The world of the unseen starts to take shape. If we can see this unseen world without fear, it will not control us and we will be liberated by our growing understanding of our natural world.

In Australia the convict settlement at Port Arthur in Tasmania is another case in point. Many people visiting the old gaol and surrounding buildings have felt very disturbed by the energy of the site and been very anxious to leave. The incredible amount of emotional distress, anger and fear felt by the convicts sentenced to spend time in Port Arthur has not simply 'gone away', it remains in the energy of the buildings and the land. This strong energy may well have been a factor that precipitated the recent massacre there.

Imbalances

Another significant element that affects the environment and the flow of Qi or life force through that environment is what I call Disturbed Nature Consciousness, where, by dowsing, we can detect an imbalance in the Yin and Yang aspects of the energy field. Too much Yang (or 'active' energy) leads to hyperactivity or an inability to relax or to heightened nervous tension and over-tiredness. At the other end of the scale – and far more prominent – is excessive Yin energy. A high Yin energy creates an unhealthy environment which produces an atmosphere of little or no motivation for those living in that energy field. As a result of the draining effect of the high Yin value the immune system suffers and consequently many health problems can be aggravated where this type of energy prevails.

In general, Geo-physical causes create an imbalance in the Yin/Yang energies. Technology, with its electrical or microwave radiation, is likely to cause an excessive Yang state in a building. A major factor in excessive Yin energy in a building is metaphysical disturbance. Having dowsed several hundred buildings I have found that where a negative thread exists there is a corresponding drop in the Yang energy of the building. It is as if these areas of disturbance are drawing on the energy of the environment in order to maintain their own limited integrity.

Some buildings draw heavily on the natural high energy spots in an environment. High energy spots can be detected by the energy dowser as expanding spirals as opposed to the reducing spiral of the draining energy pattern. On several sites I found that once a draining energy pattern has been cleared, the energy of a room where the disturbance was located will return to a natural high energy state. The disturbing energy pattern appears to be aware of the high energy spot and is taking advantage of it. The more disturbing patterns there are in a building and the greater the intensity of those patterns the higher will be the Yin value. A high Yin figure means that the environment will be more draining for anyone living in that space. Excessive Yin values are not good for business ventures. A higher Yang value needs to be sought for business success.

The Consciousness Factor

I have been in many houses in which the Qi energy does not enter. Sometimes the Qi will not even come in through the front gate. There are times when an energy field prevents the

Qi from flowing freely. This energy field may be a result of geological faulting pressure, though this is rare. It might be the result of an artifact having a very powerful negative impact on its surroundings or the householder might even be responsible. When someone has suffered either physically or emotionally, they tend to create a barrier around themselves to stop them from being hurt again. This barrier can even extend to the perimeters of the house and affect the flow of not only unwanted energies, but also positive and life giving energy as well.

But more often than not the cause for such a broad area of disturbance is the very consciousness of the land. For whatever reason the 'spirit' of the land, its consciousness, can be damaged. The obvious reasons for this state could include people's lack of sensitivity when dealing with the environment. Large earthworks adversely affect the energy patterns of the earth, as do dams, cities, railway lines, high tension power lines and so on. Naturally occurring disturbances include earthquakes, plate movement, volcanic activity and geological fault lines. Moreover there are other energies which impact upon the environment in addition to these gross physical aspects. We have looked already at metaphysical disturbance and seen how it can affect people living in disturbed areas. Having realised the impact that metaphysical disturbance has on the flow of the Qi energy or life force through an environment and how that environment can respond after the disturbing pattern is cleared, it is a simple step to see how the natural environment is affected.

If we liken the stress in the environment to how we, as physical human beings, deal with stress, it is easy to see how the physical environment can be adversely affected. When a person undergoes a traumatic experience without 'trauma counselling', evidence of that trauma can manifest many years later. This is particularly true if the person was unable at the time of the trauma to express the pain and grief the event caused: "It is not the traumas we suffer in childhood which makes us emotionally ill but the inability to express the trauma"[16].This experience locks the memory away, affecting that person's life in some way or other, often for years. Similarly, the earth can store trauma. A disturbing event, be it of a physical nature, emotional, mental or spiritual lays down an imprint in the subtle energy field of the earth. If this imprint has enough energy behind it, or the damaging effect is maintained, then the traumatised area is affected more deeply and for a greater period of time, as is the case in certain cultures involving human sacrifice, torture or execution sites. Human fear and misery set up particular vibrations that disturb the surrounding energy fields. The more such emotions occur in one particular area, the more likely it is that the energy of the earth will store those disturbing frequencies.

'Elemental' Energies

An interesting observation around such areas where significant trauma has been stored on the physical environment is the complete absence of elemental energies such as fairies, devas, sprites and angelic beings who are all members of the hierarchy of our natural environment. Whether we accept the existence of these elemental energies or not is a personal matter but many people with whom I speak tell stories of their observations of these energies. Others deny their existence, primarily because they have not seen them. In the West there is a saying "I'll believe it when I see it". Wayne Dyer has a novel approach to this saying, one far closer to the truth in my opinion, "You'll see it when you believe it"[17]. Madame Curie could not see the radioactivity that she worked with although she knew that something was happening. Regrettably the energy that she could not see and scarcely understood finally took her life.

When the spirit of the land has been damaged, a 'cloud' or ' fog' descends over that area. This 'fog' is comprised of low frequency vibrations which create a heavy energy pattern. Its pattern prevents the Qi from flowing freely and harmoniously through the environment at the same time it also drives out energy patterns of a higher, more 'delicate' frequency, including nature sprites, fairies, elves, devas and angelic beings.

From our human perspective the result is similar to the nightclub experience I related previously. A sensitive person could not live in such an environment without being adversely affected by it. The energy is too disturbing and creates more tension and imbalance in anyone trying to spend time in such an area. So it is with areas where the consciousness of the land has been disturbed. Energies, human or otherwise, will be affected. The more sensitive the being the more obvious is the disturbance to them. Hence natural elemental energies with a high degree of sensitivity are the first to experience the adverse effects of disturbance in their environment. In severe cases I have found a complete absence of these elemental energies. The earth is crying out for help. Only when balance is restored can the elemental energies return. As we move down the scale of sensitivity so more and more beings become aware of the disturbing energy pattern. Without an awareness of the cause of the disturbance the fears of those affected add to the power of the fog; and instead of helping to enlighten the environment they perpetuate the disturbance.

Areas of this type of disturbance can affect one house or a whole neighbourhood. Low energy areas of a depressed physical, emotional, mental or spiritual type, even blocked financial energy, can be the result of this type of disturbance. As we become more aware of the existence of this type of energy field we are more empowered to restore harmony. Fortunately many of the factors which created these areas no longer supply energy to the disturbed areas and are easy to clear. The difference in an environment cleared of these patterns is remarkable.

Whilst working on a house in the hinterland of the Sunshine Coast I encountered a disturbance of this nature. My clients had owned the property for three years but had only recently completed the house. Despite an affinity with the land there were some aspects of the environment which my clients found most uncomfortable. It was difficult for them to put into words the nature of their uneasiness. Whilst dowsing and tuning into the cause, I felt that the current owners had some unfinished business, on some level, with the local peoples of the area and that this had created considerable stress in the environment. As this thought came into my mind, a wind came up and slammed doors throughout the house. (I have been working in this field for too long to have any belief left in chance events.)

After focussing energy into the disturbing pattern I 'felt' that the pattern had cleared. This feeling was followed quickly by a picture of a celebration of the earlier inhabitants of the area: a corroboree. There were a few other areas requiring attention and they passed easily with no more wind or goosebumps. That afternoon, whilst I was working at the husband's office on the coast, he had a phone call from his wife who was still at the house. She said that thousands of birds had arrived and flown twice around the perimeter of the 25 hectares of their land, something that had never happened before (nor since to my knowledge). Believing in the strong inter-connectivity of all life it was not possible for me to think that this was a random event. Once harmony is restored to an environment all life knows [18]. When the light shines on one pearl all the others know about it immediately, according to the Web of Indra. The birds, just as much a part of this holoverse as we are, knew that harmony had been restored and came to celebrate.

Similarly, whilst working on a motel that had a considerable number of problems, I dowsed a strong disturbance originating in the restaurant. Which had a cold, nasty feel. The young staff would not go there after dark on their own. They thought it was haunted. There was no ghost there, only a disturbed energy pattern which was the consciousness of the land. Business picked up after it was cleared. Likewise there was a low turnover service station which had a similar problem in one of the sheds behind the pumps. Once this was cleared business picked up. Similarly a Hotel/Public House running at a crippling loss had severe disturbances in the environment; when balance was restored, the takings increased remarkably.

All life is influenced by such energies, whether we are aware of it or not. It is not just elemental energies that feel the heaviness of a disturbed environment. All levels of life are affected because all levels are connected and are ultimately one.

11

Dowsing One to One

Unlocking Personal Patterns

In chapter 1, I explored the various subtle energy bodies encompassing the physical world and the part they played, via the chakra system, in receiving and transmitting higher frequencies. When dowsing with the 'L' rod on these energy fields we are led to areas corresponding to a blockage or resistance in either the physical or subtle bodies. Using the pendulum it is possible to discover in which subtle bodies the disturbance is located. These patterns are indications of stress, on one level or another, that is currently manifesting, or will become obvious at some point in the future. Such patterns, particularly in the subtle bodies, have a harmful effect on a person. That any of these patterns exist in the first place is detrimental to the overall well-being of the individual. By maintaining a clear and balanced energy pattern in the subtle bodies there is less chance of any physical distress occurring for that person. The longer these patterns remain locked into the subtle energy fields the more likely they are to create a physical manifestation resulting in disease. The patterns are locked into a person's consciousness by the attachment which he or she has formed with the memory of the experience. That experience could be in conscious memory or be so distant or painful that consciousness has shut out the memory. If the memory has lasted for a long time and no resolution has been reached then the dynamic tension will be very powerful.

When dowsing on these patterns it is possible that either the client or the dowser will receive a picture or a feeling related to the particular disturbance currently being worked on. However, because some of the patterns are still too sensitive to be dealt with, any 'healing' will result from removing the patterns layer by layer, like the layers of an onion. Each time a new layer is exposed, the fundamental cause rises closer and closer to the surface. Without confusing patterns dominating a person's perceptions it becomes easier to access deeper causes, thus bringing the person closer to healing on a fundamental level.

Releasing Stress

It is important to state here that I do not heal. I might facilitate healing and be an important part in a healing process, but I do not heal. I cannot encourage a person to release stored memory that they are not ready to deal with, nor can I wipe the slate clean of karma or obscurations for someone deeply enmeshed in a confused reality. However, as explained previously, it is possible to work towards a point where a person is ready to present a fundamental cause and is ready to see the recurring patterns of karmic influences and release them.

Where the environment is disturbed, by whatever means, our bodies will be affected by that stress. If we spend too long in a stressed environment we will become increasingly and adversely affected by that stress. We will also create stress in our life, apart from the stress that may or may not exist in the external environment. Our stressed state will then influence the environment, so much so that it will reflect that stress back to us or others in the environment.

At this stage it is important to spend some time examining the potential causes of stress for which we are personally responsible.

The Stress of Memory

We are in fact bodies of energy which can be as fluid and plastic as modelling clay responding instantly to the sculptor's hands (that is to our higher minds, thoughts and emotional energy). The more we understand this concept then the easier it becomes for us to regain a degree of control over the reality that manifests via our physical body.

In an earlier chapter we saw how the physical body is the manifestation, via the chakra system, of information stored in the DNA, namely karmic patterns and information received and transmitted via the subtle bodies. Where discord is evident in any of these sub-systems (DNA, Karma or subtle bodies as memory) then ultimately physical manifestations such as dis-ease, sickness, emotional or mental dis-harmony become apparent.

Because we are physical beings we are kept operational by our memories. Each cell works on memory, reproducing according to the memory stored fundamentally in the DNA. Since we have a physical body with which to experience life on earth, our experiences are inseparable from the memories of our DNA. As we go through life we gather memories of life experiences and store them up, thereby building a future based on those memories. The fact that memories go way beyond that which we could have physically experienced in one life time indicates a continuity of thought, consciousness and memory transfer that supports multiple existences. One such personal experience was my own understanding of Buddhist concepts and my ability to discuss deep philosophical matters with Buddhist monks before I had read anything on the subject whatsoever. Where did this information come from? Why me? How is it possible that a young child can play classical piano like a master? Why do some people get sick when we all start out very much the same? Why are some people happy and some sad, or some are at peace and some at war?

The Source and Force of Memory

It is important to examine how we access memories, where they come from and how they shape the experiences we have on earth this time round.

I have already touched upon consciousness being beyond time and space as we know it [19], which is an important notion since the application of this knowledge (or better still a direct knowing) provides a number of answers to otherwise unanswerable questions. For the sake of our limited linear understanding we need to take a point from which to begin this journey. Whatever point is chosen will be in consciousness somewhere, (because nothing exists outside of consciousness) and will provide a foundation upon which to build an understanding of the bigger picture.

With the understanding that consciousness is beyond time and space it is difficult to imagine there was a beginning and that there might be an end to creation. There is only changing form: energy into matter, matter into energy. The earth may have not existed at some point in time and it may not exist at another point in time. It is not the earth that is the creator. The earth only contains the creator as consciousness and supports life as we know it but it is not the centre of the universe, contrary to popular opinion. Nor are we as the inhabitants of the earth the pinnacle of life, which is an arrogant assertion that has involved people in all sorts of trouble.

When we see that energy is behind all life, and that energy is consciousness, and we fully accept that all the different species on this planet see reality in a different way, then we start to learn that there is more to the bigger picture than we are able to see. Before I began dowsing and exploring more of this unseen world, I had feelings which were inexplicable, based as they were upon my limited understanding at the time. Some of these feelings were confusing. Some were fearful. Many resulted in high anxiety. Had someone told me that in the near future I would be dowsing on consciousness I would have shook my head in amazement. I would not have laughed at them since it is not in my nature to laugh at others or my own potential, even though I was not ready to accept that potential. Now, more and more people who even a year ago would have not given me the time of day were I to discuss what I know now about consciousness are open and ready to listen. Times are changing. People who are ready are changing too. This ability to change has always been a prerequisite to evolution. Our times are no different. In fact the need to change and the inability to do so is a major factor in strife and struggle, sickness, disease, war and unrest. Yet why do some change easily whilst others resist change?

The Seed of Consciousness (Memory)

The seed of growth is an idea, a desire to experience, to learn and to grow, to explore and create, but not yet in physical form. There are many opportunities to experience and grow in the universe. Earth is one very special place and is called a free will planet. It is also a place where you can forget completely who you really are and therefore have the chance to go fully into duality and experience unique aspects of life that are not available elsewhere. One of the hazards of such a beautiful planet is that it can become addictive and we can completely forget who we truly are.

In relation to the 'seed' of consciousness, it must be recognised firstly that consciousness itself is beyond time as we know it and that consciousness is seen as the foundation from which physical life manifests, like the string that supports the pearls. Without the string, each pearl is completely alone, still beautiful no doubt but no longer a part of the whole. This is not to say that consciousness is linear. Consciousness has no beginning nor does it have an end. Consciousness is not thread-like: it just is. Consciousness is the 'cosmic soup'; we are swimming in consciousness. All matter is energy in different manifestations; likewise all energy is consciousness. God, if you will, is consciousness; therefore we are swimming in 'god'; consequently we are 'god'. The principles of the holographic universe, namely the holoverse, explain this concept in more scientific terms such as the implicate and explicate orders: that which is manifest (explicate) and that which is not (implicate). Whether energy manifests as physical or not does not affect the consciousness that is behind form and consciousness, which we otherwise call energy.

The seed then is an idea in the unmanifest (implicate) order without physical form. The force that impels the seed onward in its search for greater knowing is the creative principle of desire which seeks out a physical experience in third dimensional earth space/time. Because the seed is in the implicate order and exists outside time and space as we know it, the point in linear earth space/time that the seed chooses to enter the experience of physical form is not ruled by our mental, limited linear concepts. This means that the seed can enter a human experience in the 20th century or the 18th century, the 2nd century, even the 14th century BC if it chooses. This choice seems to be available only in the early stages of the seeds desire to experience earth space/time.

When the seed does take a physical form, which can be seen as a stepped down frequency pattern, the energy of the physical realm can be both confusing and frightening. Because the seed is new to the physical and loses its memory of who and what it was before taking on physical form, it gets caught up in the unfolding drama that is life on earth.

The Seed as Form

Throughout its experiences in a physical body, the seed, which is the core of a being, becomes more and more embroiled in life's experience. It not only attracts experiences to it but generates future experiences by its desire to explore. Certain energetic tensions develop in the collective 'seed' and body. Memories are stored in the cellular structure of the physical form and in the more subtle energy bodies associated with that physical form. As pure awareness, the seed's consciousness knows neither right nor wrong, good or bad, hot or cold, light or dark: it just 'is'. But its physical, emotional and mental experiences in physical form are quite a different thing. Likes and dislikes develop and cause friendships and/or enmity. Once the physical form is no longer able to function and dies, the seed might remembered its true nature and free itself from the illusion. This does not mean that by freeing itself the seed no longer seeks experiences and evolution on this plane of existence. More accurately it could, if it wished, continue to gain experience, but it always remembers its true nature. 'If it wished' is a key phrase because it implies free will. The alternative is a continuation of the dream state which seems to affect most embodying souls with their emotional attachment to issues that, whilst in physical form, the consciousness judges as good or bad or right or wrong, will only ensure an enforced return to the physical plane.

Emotional attachment acts like a magnet for the seed, drawing it back into physical form to experience some more of the same, or to play a different role. Once back in physical form the seed again loses its memory of its true nature. Greater ranges of opposites are experienced, thus drawing the seed deeper and deeper into the game of physical life. Experiences create more and more tension within the being as these experiences accumulate to produce greater light or greater darkness. Neither is right or wrong to the seed, but the essence of the seed is slowly pushed into the background as the physical, mental and emotional aspects take over.

The Seed and Memory

The tensions of duality expand the seed's choices of where and when to take on physical form but in effect these choices in themselves become more limited and increasingly linear in relation to earth, space and time. In each intervening period, between physical forms, the seed is drawn by the desires of the body into more duality and more experiences instead of remembering itself. This drawing or 'pulling' creates a dynamic tension: on one hand it expands the knowledge base of the seed; on the other hand it binds the seed more strongly to experiences in a physical form. In Eastern terms this state of tension created by an addiction to duality is called karma, which is the law of cause and effect. As the seed forgets its 'self' and seeks to experience anger, power, lust, sensual delights, poverty, slavery, freedom, the life of the warrior, the knight, the maiden, the priestess, the sorcerer and so on, the very desire for more experiences ensures that the seed will return to a physical form.

It becomes increasingly difficult for the seed to remember itself as it accumulates more and more karma. Tension binds it to the 'wheel', that is, the wheel of becoming, of birth, life and death (as expressed in Buddhist terms). It is also difficult for the seed to awaken if the very nature of life on earth is designed to prevent that awakening. Many 'seeds' currently in body form on earth have had untold numbers of experiences in physical form. The more experiences they have had, the more their perceptions of this world seem real and absolute. Memories accrued over many experiences become set in the mind of the 'seed's' projection, namely the physical body. When a memory becomes a set pattern then all other 'realities' are affected or are created because they are based upon that perception. Moreover, the way that these patterns are formed becomes one of the limiting factors that dictate when and where the seed can take on physical form and the experiences that the physical form will undergo.

Note that we are drawn into the experience of living as opposed to experiencing life from a place of clear knowing of who and what we are. Freedom of will is limited by the dictates of the body's relationship to its external environment and to other seeds which are heavily disguised as human beings. If we were to remember who we were then we would never behave as we do to one another, for their sakes and for our own. We could never abuse our planet if we truly understood the symbiotic relationship that we as physical beings have with this planet.

Growth Needs Patience and Understanding

If you are unable to accept this information at this point in time have patience with yourself. Everyone has varying degrees of selective hearing, seeing and being. Our readiness to accept information is due partly to our attachment or repulsion to previous experiences and memories and how we react to those memories. Accepting that our lifespan is three score years and ten is a myth and is a great denial and excuse for abusing others and the planet. Look beyond this debilitating limitation to see the future. There are many futures available – if we make the right choice now we will empower ourselves on the road to freedom. If we build up great attachment to memories, whether emotional or physical or even to the memories we repel, we will remain locked into duality thereby ensuring we never experience the oneness of being and the true nature of self.

Life is like the pebble that turned into a wall. From the tiniest seed an incredibly complex and involved scenario unfolds. The movie comes to life and we forget that we created the movie and are not just characters in it. An interesting aspect of the pebble analogy is that the more we believe in the pebble influencing everything that we do, the bigger the pebble gets and the bigger it gets then the more influence it has and so on. But if for one moment we stopped believing in the pebble; (the rock or wall or mountain) and however much energy we put into it up to that point in time, one of two things will happen. If the energy put into the pebble was indeed great and we stored up memory as tension in the physical, emotional, mental or spiritual bodies, then that tension will need to be released by precipitating a healing crisis beyond one's wildest imaginings. The healing crisis associated with it could then result in physical death. However keep in mind that although the physical will die anyway, it is better to heal the tensions that create the need for a healing crisis in the first place. At least that way, when the seed seeks physical expression again, it will be that much closer to remembering who and what it is, thus avoiding the need for such a severe healing crisis next time round.

The other thing that could happen is that through your non-attachment to the events that pass as reality on this planet you simply wake up and remember who and what you are. This result is both desirable and possible. It is not my belief that we have to process our past, that is, mull over our memories and re-live our experiences until the need for a healing crisis is created As we believe, so we are.

Similarly I believe that we are not earthbound and limited by the physical nature of the body. The idea of physical limitation has been supported and nurtured over the ages to prevent us from remembering just how powerful we are. A side effect of this 'dogma' has been that we have experienced events of a truly diverse nature. But the dogma's exponents have also created the dynamic tension needed to propel the seed into awakening. In effect, the dogma is a double edged sword; it was originally designed to maintain a particular status quo, but by its very nature, provides the means by which the seeds can re-awaken. However, none of us are 'there' yet. There are still so many 'karmic' 'attachments' and limiting belief patterns that while many people believe they still have to process their experiences, others are still addicted to the belief that they 'are' their memories.

Of Memory and Awareness

Certain memories, no matter how old or how recent, tend to dominate who we think we are. These memories, by their very nature, keep the situation surrounding the memory alive and ensure that we spend the next millennia trying to overcome the memory. But what is a memory and why do we react so strongly to some memories and seem to ignore others?

By accumulating experiences and moving further away from our true self, the experiences become more real. As the memories of experiences build up, we develop an attachment or a revulsion to those memories. Consequently this duality draws us back to more of the same experience ("perhaps it will be better next time round"; "maybe I'll get my own back"). Always some more, never enough – it is the same with an individual life, always wanting more and never satisfied. The state of never having enough is aggravated by the incorrect perception of who we are. If we could remember only a small part of our true nature then we would always be satisfied.

The way we judge others and ourselves displays our lack of awareness of our true nature. We are deeply caught up in this life and the 'reality' it presents. By judging others, or ourselves, we are responsible for the degree of attachment or revulsion to certain memories from our past. It appears to be quite fashionable to blame our past for who we are now. I could state that I had a disturbed childhood with a dysfunctional family and that my father was an alcoholic, but we have all had dysfunctional pasts (he was not and I did not). We have all experienced abuse, if not personally then through the collective consciousness that is the cosmic soup, be it in this life's experience or a different one. If we think that we are our memories then we become victims of those memories. It is our attachment to the memory that is the problem. The moment we accept the memory as a part of our past and as one of our learning experiences and forgive ourselves for having had that experience, even forgiving any person whom we felt was guilty of inflicting that experience upon us, then we are closer to being able to remember who we truly are.

The Moment That Matters

The memories of our experiences are the reason for this physical life. The memories are not us but they may however assist us to become better and more aware 'seeds'. Then we will start to redraw the picture and re-connect with the greater reality. Only then can we understand the true value of the myriad of memories we have gathered and grow from the experience and not let it limit us.

Some people let a memory (good or bad) to which they are 'addicted' through guilt, anger, hate, fear, lust or love play over and over again like a video. All other experiences that follow are built upon the foundation of one good or bad memory, often from childhood. Thus the pebble turns into a wall. However if through a better understanding we deal with the issue whilst it is still a pebble, life will take on a totally different meaning. Becoming aware that we are replaying the same video over and over empowers us to do something about it. At first the task appears too great to take the video out of the VCR and file it out of harm's way. We can become so addicted to that video and so caught up in believing it to be real that we create a state of powerful tension around that memory.

Often we are unable to recall specific details of certain memories because the pain associated with the memory is so strong or so distant. In this instance it is difficult to access the memory in order to see how it has created our lives, let alone work on releasing the memory. We are, after all, creatures of habit. How and when we learned specific habits may be lost in time yet we still follow them. Those habits are our security blankets protecting us from the unknown, or, as Nelson Mandela said, "from our own brilliance and power".

Awareness Means Responsibility

If we believe that we are victims of circumstance, we then logically feel that there is someone or something to blame for our perceived condition. This thought only serves to keep us in duality and prevents us from facing the fact that we are totally responsible for who we are, what we experience and how we relate to those experiences. It also ensures that we are caught up in the need to process our past in order to be better members of society today, or to evolve beyond that which we interpret as limitations to what we are currently experiencing.

When we know that we are powerful, talented and enlightened and see others around us struggling with their past by playing the same song over and over again, we cannot say to them: "you are powerful, brilliant, gorgeous, talented and enlightened", if they are so caught up in their own drama that they cannot even hear what we are saying. Nor can we judge them for who they are and what they are doing.

A friend recently saw a pattern that had existed between her and many female friends for many years. I said that I recalled telling her this two and a half years ago. "Yes", she said, "but why couldn't I see it then?"

12

Awakening To Reality

There are conservative members of the 'old school' who know of the world of alternative medicine but are not yet ready to accept the major shift in belief patterns that will allow them to accept such information. They might even deny ever hearing of it, despite repeated attempts by friends to 'enlighten' them. Yet months or even years later, as a result of being a part of the cosmic soup within which all unfolds, they will have been influenced to a sufficient degree by the growing awareness within the soup and a light will come on. Then it is their turn to tell their friends of their discovery, indeed those same friends that had tried to 'enlighten' them before.

There is no right or wrong here, no better or worse, no holier than thou: just karma and obscurations. Some of us have more karma and obscurations than others depending how long we have been caught up in the pursuit of worldly experience and how attached we are to those experiences.

When I awoke to the importance of memories and the part they played in the unfolding of our realities I began to see the connection of energies manifesting in the physical, emotional, mental and spiritual environments with the belief patterns of those living in that environment. This connection applies to families, villages, towns, cities, states, nations, continents, races, religions and planets. Various environments attract particular types of person, animal or plant-life because of the energy characteristics of a particular environment. Likewise various people, animals or plant-life enhance certain environments, enabling the pattern, or habit to become established over millennia.

If a healthy person moves into an unhealthy environment something has to change. In my experience a person generally succumbs to the energy of the environment. Occasionally I have been told by a client, "What am I doing here? This environment is so hostile!". As the person becomes more aware of the reason, whatever it may be, for living in such an area, so that area either has less of a hold over them or the energy changes to better suit the client. Depressed neighbour-hoods for example, seem to be self perpetuating and unless something is done to stabilise such a situation on a very basic level, no amount of money or aid will solve the problem. It is as though the problem is a part of the total environment and until the right questions are asked no solutions will be forthcoming.

Taking Personal Responsibility

Today when I look at factors of a geo-physical, metaphysical or even technological nature that appear to be disturbing influences in the lives of clients, I look particularly at the part the client plays in the overall drama. How is the client responsible for creating this reality, I ask myself, knowing that any original cause may be so far back in time or space that any connection between cause and effect has been well and truly lost. No one would willingly or consciously create a hard time for themselves and everyone wants to be happy, wealthy and disease free. At the same time, people in poverty, bondage or civil war do not put themselves there on purpose but it happens all the time. A big argument against unity consciousness is that of victim consciousness: "we had no say" or "we are victims of our environment". Denial of self responsibility brought about by our willingness to let others run our lives for us leads us further into dependence upon others. Whether those others have integrity or not is questionable. Most of those to whom we turn for support and guidance are certainly not clear of their own obscurations nor in a karma free state, so how can they guide us?

There is another part of the selectivity of information, namely failing to tune in to broadcasts that are of a frequency beyond our capacity to deal with them. It is not as if we are negligent or in error. It is simply because our system which tunes into information is limited. It is as like having a radio which can receive AM broadcasts only. Without updating the model there is no way that we can receive broadcasts from it on the FM band. If we were to try and tune into information that was beyond our capacity to receive, like putting two thousand volts through a television set, we would blow a fuse. We need to consciously fine tune our systems in order to access safely the information on the other band. This information has always been available. It does not mean that it does not exist because we are not tuned into it. All information is available to us provided we have the ability to receive it. There are many different ways of accessing this information, but, as Wayne

Dyer said, "You'll see it when you believe it"[20]. If our mind is not able to deal with the quantum shift in perceptions required to hold a new frequency then we must proceed slowly and gently in letting go of old limiting perceptions, piece by piece.

The Personal Benefits of Dowsing

I have found dowsing to be a great help in accessing information at various levels. Not only has the act of dowsing allowed me to access more levels of information and to consciously fine tune my own system so that greater levels may be reached, it has also provided me with a tool to help others access information by releasing the old limiting patterns.

When working with people it is only possible, in my experience, to work within their defined areas. A client with a cancer manifesting in the stomach region asked me to check the energy fields in her house. Having completed the work we then turned to look at any disturbing patterns she may be holding onto that could be responsible for her disease. Whilst dowsing the subtle energy bodies with the dowsing rod I was drawn into an area in the emotional body that was in direct alignment with the cancer. As I 'tuned' in to the disturbance I started to shiver and feel energy moving through me in wave-like formation. As I experienced this my client said, "My father is here". He had been dead for many years but she felt his presence. By now my body was shaking visibly. "Yes", I replied, "I know." When I asked (via the pendulum) what the energy of the father wanted, a word came strongly into my mind. That word was forgiveness. "Do you wish to forgive?" I asked, "No" came the reply. "To ask for forgiveness?" I questioned. "Yes", replied my client's father. I conveyed this information to my client who burst out crying, understanding exactly what was going on. It related to a childhood trauma, unresolved for many years and like a thorn in my client's side: a thorn that eventually caused a physical symptom to manifest. Yet our removal of the thorn did not clear the cancer. It did however give the client an opportunity to heal herself of the disease. Had the thorn been removed much earlier it is quite possible that the cancer might never have manifested.

When an issue that lies deep within an individual's energy patterning is untreated, and especially if that issue has enough negative emotion around it, then physical symptoms are inevitable. Once the body shows signs of physical distress then the work of rebalancing the energy becomes more difficult. It is easier and more effective to treat potential physical distress than it is to work with manifesting disease. If the body takes on a negative pattern, not only do we have to look for an initial cause but we must also re-educate the body as well.

Breaking Negative Patterns

Dealing with migraine is a good example of re-educating our body in order to break negative energy patterns. There are many medical and 'alternative' descriptions of what migraine is and why it occurs but very little questioning about why it occurs. Medical questions are limited in their extent and may only list stress as a prime factor beyond the clinical explanations. But why should one body be stressed when another, with a similar workload, relationships and financial issues not be stressed? When I have dowsed for migraine sufferers a common factor is trauma and tension in the emotional energy body. By sympathetic resonance it is relatively easy to reduce the emotional stress in the client.

A friend once asked me to talk with a woman in her mid forties who had been suffering migraine attacks every two days since childhood. I spent 45 minutes with that person, who, by the way, had little or no idea what I did and consequently little faith in my work. She had sought relief from many different sources for years but to no avail. Later that day she reported feeling more tired than usual. She said she was under a lot of pressure in her life and that this was a factor adding to the migraine but one which she was not ready to do anything about. The following night she had a major emotional release. The migraine attacks reduced frequency to one every ten days after that. She came back to see me just once more.

In another case, (again a referral) a woman who was returning home via our house was in great pain with the onset of a severe migraine attack. She did not wait for a treatment, stating she had to get home before it got worse. Later that evening she rang me, explaining that her pain had increased and asked for help. I started dowsing (keep in mind that dowsing is beyond time and space so distance is of little consequence). She told me later that the pain had increased after the dowsing, becoming extremely severe and that she had gone straight to bed. Later she reported a reduced incidence of migraine attack, from one every two days to one every ten days. When I worked with that client again no more emotional issues showed up as they had in the first visit. In fact, on the first visit it was only emotional issues that presented themselves. Obviously, when working with someone in pain the first issue is to alleviate the immediate cause for the pain. On the second visit, still dealing with the fundamental cause of the migraine, we discussed issues in the mental and spiritual energy fields. We drew closer to the core issue with each visit. At the time of writing this is an ongoing case.

Negating Disturbances

It is interesting to note that in a strong disturbance there can be a sequence of the spiral patterns, all in line with a particular point in the physical where distress is manifesting. One is in the emotional body; one corresponds to the mental body; another is in the spiritual and yet another in the GAIA field. It appears that the original cause for any manifest disturbance starts in the outer energy bodies, in this case the GAIA field, which is the bridge between spirit and matter (between the seed and the physical form) and is fundamental to who we think we are and contains information that goes well beyond any physical experience. These are experiences that pre-date any memory we have gained whilst in the physical. In a sense this is pre-physical memory which fundamentally affects who and what we think we are and how we relate to this physical experience. If we carry such memory patterns and they are of significant importance then they affect our whole existence in the physical. The longer we deal with these issues, for example by running away from them or putting them in the too hard basket or simply denying they exist, the harder it is to bring about a release of our held-in tension.

Like falling dominoes, a severe disturbance in the GAIA field creates a particular spiritual response that deals with certain issues on the spiritual level and sets up a pattern in the mental field. As a result of a particular mental belief we experience certain emotional responses to given situations based on that belief. An emotional response that is not of a higher, or more aware frequency will have an adverse and distressing effect on the physical body. By the time this state has manifested in the physical a lot of work is required to restore balance to all levels.

Memory and Disease

After observing many patterns of illness (using the above model) I realise now that any manifestation of sickness or disease is based on memory. Imagine that inside you, at the very core of your being, a brilliant light is shining. This light has always been there, and always will be there. It is not however a very demanding light. Under 'normal' circumstances the light is content just to be there, whether you are aware of it or not. The light is constant, not transitory like this physical form and is connected to the very source of your being. For a time you may well have remembered this light is within you but, due to frequent exposure to a low rate of vibration (which we call third dimensional reality), the light has been forgotten. As memory of the light fades, generally by our addiction to the experiences offered on this planet, we forget that the light exists and even strongly deny its presence. The light is still there, of course. We cannot 'be' without it.

The more experiences we are attracted to in this 3D world and the more we become involved in the belief that this world alone is real, the light is no longer recognised as the core of our being. Our memory of the light is still there (we can never lose our memories because we are our memories), but the light is buried so deeply beneath our new memories that we can no longer access it. Consequently the beliefs that we have fallen into become our reality and over the passage of time (earth time) we add more and more reality to those beliefs. The very nature of the planetary vibration that is created by our major collective belief patterns forces us further into believing that reality to be real. On the contrary, reality is relative to the observer. If more than one person believes in a particular reality, together they add their own powers of creativity to that belief. The more people there are who believe in any one reality then the more momentum that reality gains until their power makes that reality self sustaining.

Social Disturbances

If we trace the development of earlier civilisations we can see that certain rules evolved. Perceptions of the leaders of society became the beliefs of the masses. Spiritual and religious organisations came into being, as did political movements, guilds and financial centres.

Today's major religious institutions began with a small group of people believing in a set of concepts and these organisations have now evolved over the millennia. I am not referring here to spirituality but to organised religions, which is a different area altogether. The two should fit together but delivering liberating truth has never been a strong point of religious organisations. Spirituality is the road to realisation of the truth and in our case, a remembering of the light within.

Religions became like any other hierarchical organisations and were centred around a few zealous individuals wanting to impose their perceptions on ever greater numbers, in order to create a strong power base. Those who accepted the tenets of the few leaders had willingly handed over their power because of the fear generated by those leaders and of the outcomes should the people not subscribe. A simple belief in crop failure, infertility and of course hell, was too strong to ignore for people who had forgotten that the light existed within themselves. Collective belief in fear and superstition was able to spread rapidly through a culture that believed it was in fundamental error and subject to the revenge of a god-like figure at any moment. What a perfect opportunity for those with self centred morals to take control of huge parts of a civilisation's consciousness!

When one perception gained enough momentum it sent itself out to bring more and more 'sheep' under its protective care, thereby increasing the power base. Of course, any group that becomes excessively powerful tends to bully other groups since this is a part of a major power play. Some groups succumb, others grow stronger in their own right and a race is on to recruit more numbers to the organisation, often at the expense of those who already subscribed.

When any organisation fails to meet the growing needs of its subscribers then disillusionment sets in. This consequence applies to all organisations: religious, political, financial, medical, agrarian or industrial. Disillusionment is especially relevant when the organisation has denied its members access to the truth. Remember the light is still within: as growing numbers become more aware of the existence of that light it takes hold and begins to spread like an infection.

Removing the Layers of Time

In order to become more aware of the light within, it is necessary to peel away layers of memory. Firstly recognise that it is memories that keep us a prisoner, not in a cell constructed by others but one of our own making. This is not an easy task because we are so conditioned that we have handed our very salvation over to others, leaving the task of guiding us through the darkness of religion, spirituality, governmental duties, legal arguments and financial nightmares to so-called specialists who are themselves lost in the darkness. It is amazing that no matter where we turn for help outside ourself and, knowing that the light is within each and every one of us, we ask someone presently in the darkness to lead us to the light. We even complain when those leading us fail to deliver the goods. Then we accuse the leaders of being ineffective, whether they be in the church or the government. This charade has continued for thousands of years. Play acting is formed upon various beliefs and perceptions. If you start by looking at your own beliefs and compartmentalising them you will see how you came to think you are, that is, who you picture yourself to be now.

In relation to religion, for example, we know that sometime, in antiquity, it did not exist. At some point in the evolution of the human species it was started by someone, then a a few people began spreading the word. As long as the word was relatively pure, no harm came and there was an expectation of wide public recognition of the light within. But as the movement grew and belief patterns expanded, the freedom associated with remembering the light within became a political nightmare. Steps were taken to remove parts of the original teaching. The word was kept in the hands of a hierarchy who then proceeded to administer the doctrine according to the political dictates of the time. Memories of the original teaching were destroyed or kept hidden with the 'secret teachings' reserved for the initiates only. Anyone who understood the real meaning of that word realised that in order to be initiated one had to go undergo a special training process to receive certain information. That training, at the discretion of the holders of the 'secret teachings', was – and still is – an indoctrination process aimed at safeguarding the hierarchy.

As certain memories are overlaid with newer patterns and are reinforced (advertising propaganda is an obvious modern day example) then consensus is influenced. A new belief pattern begins to emerge and before you realise it you are subscribing to yet another power game. We can only be led into this confusion because early memory of the light within is kept suppressed by unscrupulous parts of society that seek to control and manipulate patterns for their own reasons, and because we allow it to happen.

Everything around us and all the experiences that we attract are all issues that we encounter based upon our attraction or repulsion to certain ways of perceiving our world. Nonetheless we can choose to alter those perceptions. The 'trap' to avoid, however, is that whilst we try to change any perception we have of life from within, away from the old paradigms of our reality, we must not swap one illusion for another.

Individual Awakening

One of the methods currently employed by some individuals who seek to re-awaken us to the light within aims at blaming an event in the past for the dilemma we might be experiencing now. In order to move beyond the trauma of the past these practitioners try to bring it into the moment, work through the issue and then release it. In my view the only thing from our past that is still active and sensitive is our addiction to a memory, no more and no less, and we need to give ourselves an opportunity to move beyond the constrictions of that memory, which is of something that we have already experienced and dealt with. To empower the memory is to maintain a perception based in illusion. To seek an answer to any problem from within the paradigm that created the problem is doomed to failure. It is like the western band-aid approach to social issues. To exchange one belief pattern for another in the hope that another group, culture or religion knows better than the one we are accustomed to is to replace one blind leader with another. Unfortunately, this approach is encouraged by society because it keeps individuals in a constant state of uncertainty and always searching. Whilst searching, people cannot find a resting place where they are at one with themselves and all creation.

If we consider the example of Christ's energy and information which he taught two thousand years ago, we can see how those in control at the time resisted change, especially where any change empowered the people and could upset the balance of power. This resistance to change has happened throughout history and is still happening today. The light within, however dormant it may appear to be, will not be denied. Over many hundreds of experiences on this planet people have gone through a huge growth curve, even though not all of those experiences would be regarded as pleasant. Some people have become so addicted to certain belief patterns that they and the belief itself are completely united. This inseparable addiction has led to polarisation which, when threatened, immediately goes into defence mode but is followed quickly by attack. Anything that threatens an established belief by offering change is resisted. Not only is there polarisation on an individual basis but this polarisation extends to our whole picture of reality.

When one section of the planetary community desires change, another resists. Both sections think they are right and feel the need to impose their desires on the other. The result is conflict. Change of some sort is therefore inevitable. At all times change is occurring on a level where no change is truly sustainable. This is ideal for those who think they are in control and somehow immune to what happens in the rest of the system. They think that their position of power guarantees them security from the chaos they are creating. On the other hand we can scarcely point any finger of blame when we allow ourselves to be manipulated. If we blame any one or any thing else for our own shortcomings we fall again into the duality trap that holds us securely in the prison cell of our own making.

Aiming To Restore Balance

When I work on the energy in a house or in commercial premises or even in a larger section of our environment where an energy imbalance occurs, any number of things things can happen. In order to restore and hold a balanced state I must be able to hold the frequency of the disturbance without fear or judgement. I need to access a higher frequency that draws the lower, imbalanced energy field up to it. In effect, it is like bringing a powerful light to shine in dark areas. Many of the energy patterns I come across shy away from the light. A dark, fearful energy of a low vibration which resists change will seek refuge in its own limited understanding. My approach is still the same, whether it happens on the physical, individual or metaphysical level .

When a disturbing pattern of a metaphysical nature is found in any environment, the energy around that pattern is affected in an adverse way and limits the potential of the environment to achieve harmony. The disturbance, which is of a low vibration and is often fear-based, will try and escape from the lighter higher frequency energy that I represent. In the case of a metaphysical disturbance, where the cause for that pattern is no longer actively supplying the disturbing pattern with energy, it is a relatively easy matter to change the frequency from one of low energy fear vibration to a higher, more loving pattern. When the issue of fear is overcome, the energy pattern itself readily absorbs more energy thereby raising the frequency, almost willingly. Where there are many disturbing patterns in an environment, they all serve to maintain a low energy state which affects not only those people living in that environment but life on all levels whether physically manifest or not.

It could be said that where you have a 'gathering' of disturbing patterns they create a sufficiently low energy area which then attract other low level energy patterns. This 'rule' applies equally to the environment, individuals, towns, cities, continents and planets.

It is also possible that due to significant disturbances on any one of a number of levels the earth's energy itself has become so out of balance that this imbalance causes other lesser imbalances to be attracted or even occur in that vicinity. Whatever the reason, the balance of power shifts as the area is slowly restored to one of harmony.

Where negative low energy patterns existed, more light floods into the area being worked on when the frequency of the prime cause or of individual patterns is raised. As more light, or higher frequency energy patterns become prevalent, so lower frequencies are no longer able to remain in a low energy state. For a short time there may be physical signs of disturbance as the balance shifts. But the more that high energy is put into an environment the less low vibration energies can exist without change. Most low energy patterns seem to be anchored into the physical world, somehow unable to move freely about the environment. Hence they are unable to escape the higher energy and must change. Consequently the more energy they absorb the easier it is for them to change.

During the time that the higher frequencies become dominant I have discovered that many of the lesser energy patterns will make the required shift into a higher vibration of their own accord. Soon after the work starts, the process of balance becomes quite automatic and no longer depends upon my involvement. The same thing happens within an individual in the same way.

Proceed Calmly

Perhaps when reading through this book you might have declared: "this is all very well but how am I going to be able to achieve this other state, this new perspective?" Relax. It is happening for you, by you, with or without your conscious help. Let me explain this statement as I understand it.

The light which is the higher frequency energy is ever present. You could not be without it. Over the millennia of earth time various experiences have combined to deny the light. The darker (lower frequency) energy patterns have taken over and now govern our conscious process. Without some form of assistance it is possible that we will stay locked into the belief patterns generated and supported by the lower level energy patterns. Help is at hand. Not everyone today is lost in the lower energy levels and the limiting patterns these lower levels support. There have been times throughout the history of the evolution of consciousness when individuals have broken through the controlling factors of their own personality and the fears contained therein. They offered themselves to the greater good of the whole. As Nelson Mandela said: "and as we let our own light shine, we unconsciously give other people permission to do the same. As we are liberated from our own fear, our presence automatically liberates others".

For those who are deep within the earth experience, a multitude of different experiences have moulded their consciousness to accept and participate in consensus reality. For some people, the act of allowing the light to shine out – even the remembering of the light's existence – may be something that appears to be so far out of reach that to gain it this time around is impossible. That is not so. Others who have listened more to their inner instinctual voices, rather than to the intellectuals who reason over the more recent life experiences, know that the light is within and is close to the conscious mind. These people are more open and ready for change.

Then there are people who are less caught up in the dramas being played out at the present time and therefore are more easily able to access the inner light. To recognise who is coming from the inner light and who is coming from an egocentric place is a key issue. I mentioned previously in the section on channelling, that not all of the information comes from a higher level of understanding and awareness. Individuals who attempt to break free of control issues and victim consciousness often experience an internal struggle between a fearful ego and the acknowledgement of the light within. As a result, any information he or she wishes to share is still coming from a place of duality and confusion. We must listen to our inner inner voices, asking: "does this feel right for me?"

Access the Inner Light

For those who are becoming more aware of the light within, keep in mind that simply by being that light you add to the brilliance of the whole, thus enabling those around you (like moths drawn to a light) to gain the beginnings of the remembering. In turn this light spreads and grows. The more it grows the more people are affected, whether they are aware of it or not.

When the inner struggle settles down and the light energy shines through the outer struggles you also calm down. Whatever we have drawn to ourselves changes. Stress falls away;, tension and sickness become things of the past. When the inner levels of being regain a balanced state, the outer manifestations return to a balanced harmonious state. On a planetary level (and because all is consciousness) we recognise that it is our polluted thoughts that have contaminated the energy of the earth. This contamination manifests itself as stress and causes an imbalance of the natural frequencies of the earth – another Catch 22 situation: the environment is making us sick and we are making the environment sick. As the earth struggles to restore and maintain a balanced state the imbalance in our consciousness is ever ready to return imbalance or chaos to the natural order.

Healing

People will help heal the planetary vibrations by coming from a high energy aware state instead of a low energy fear based on judgement and control. The balance of power is nevertheless shifting. In any process of change the established conservative orders exert more energy to try and maintain control. Their efforts will inevitably lead to more fear and greater conflicts and so they will design stronger measures to regain and keep control. The result will be great upheaval until the higher frequency energy patterns are so well established (as in the example of the home) that more and more energies that were formerly in a low energy state will start to vibrate to higher and higher patterns. For many people this shift will be quite sudden and apparently involuntary, but will gather momentum rapidly once the point of no return is reached.

When we experience a personal healing crisis and the tension causing the disorder is released, we can expect to see planetary healing. The tensions that have been held for so long will melt into higher frequencies.

Yet such global crises can be modified in the same way as we are able to modify any personal healing crisis. By accepting change rather than fighting against it, in particular by surrendering our memories rather than hanging onto them, we reduce the severity of the healing crisis. The further down the path of duality we are enmeshed, the more generated tension there is to release. So it is with the earth's consciousness. Whilst we attempt to control and manipulate the earth's energy from an imbalanced state we create more imbalance from which the planet has to recover.

Seeking

For those who seek a greater light, I recommend that you stay in the company of the brightest beings you can find. Use your power of discernment. Do not spend time with those who judge themselves and you and others nor with those who slander and ridicule you or attack or blame others or their environment. Do not remain in the company of those who are unhappy. Such people always wish they are somewhere else, whether that somewhere is in the next town, the next planet or another dimension. Your desire to reach your own truth will prevail once the seed which is already deep within you has been recognised. It will respond to a little loving care. Be aware there are many traps along the way, some of them trying to seduce you from the goal. But they are all illusion. Look beyond the illusion of time. Open your heart and mind to your personal truth and be free.

Footnotes

1   Rupert Sheldrake – morphic resonance.
The Rebirth of Nature" pp.88 - 90

2   Chapter 4. "Vibrational Medicine" by Richard Gerber is high on the list of informative materials on many aspects covered in this book as is "Hands of Light" by Barbara Ann Brennan.

3   "Cross Currents" by Robert Becker M.D.
Chapter Two, page 30

4   "The Holographic Universe" by Michael Talbot;
Chapter Two. pp 47 - 49

5   There are many names for this type of energy disturbance. A generic term commonly used in Europe is 'geo-pathic stress', a little less fear based than many of the more modern terms. Consequently geo-pathic stress is the term I shall use to refer to any areas associated with the Earth where stress is evident.

6   The subject of memory and its impact on our unfolding reality is dealy with in chapter 7 pp 63–66 and chapter 11 pp143–149

7   Undertakers are finding bodies last longer these days before decomposition sets in.

8   see 'Science of the Gods' by David Ash

9   See the intrepretation of Karma page 145

10   This concept of life is similar to the Catholic version of "putting up with suffering now because your rewards are in heaven".

*

,

[11] A process commonly known as the 100th Monkey Syndrome See "God I Am" by Peter Erbe, Chapter 3. p 45.

[12] "Psychic" is not a word I prefer since it has too many 'New Agey' connotations

[13] "A Course in Miracles" frequent references throughout the book.

[14] For more detailsed information see page 141

[15] See "Karma and Reincarnation" p. 16. Dr. Hiroshi Motoyama. (There are numerous other examples throughout the book)

[16] Reclaiming the Inner Child. Edited by J. Abrams. p 228 John Bradshaw quoting Alice Miller.

[17] From the book titled "You'll See It When You Believe It" by Wayne Dyer

[18] The Web of Indra. see page 60

[19] Consciousness beyond time and space see chapter 8 page 80

[20] From the book titled "You'll See It When You Believe It" by Wayne Dyer

Eric conducts workshops and seminars on all aspects covered in this book and is open to correspondence, the address to write to is:–

P.O. Box 751
Maroochydore
Queensland 4558
Australia